Harshel C Logan

December 1977
Mary Christmas to
Frances
from Mary and Wes

Small World, Long Gone

Avis Dungan Carlson, 1914

SMALL WORLD

...Long Gone

A Family Record of an Era

by AVIS CARLSON

THE SCHORI PRESS · 1975

Designed by Ward Schori
Printed in the United States of America
At
The Schori Press
1580 Maple Avenue, Evanston, Illinois 60201

Library of Congress Catalog Card Number 75-25212
ISBN 0-911694-00-5

First Printing November 1975

Second Printing May 1976

SMALL WORLD, LONG GONE

ILLUSTRATIONS

The woodcuts used throughout this book are by Herschel C. Logan, famous Kansas artist and engraver, who has won many awards for his outstanding depictions of Kansas scenes.

Frontispiece, photograph of Avis Dungan Carlson, 1914.

Title page, "Kansas Landscape" woodcut.

Chapter One headpiece, page 1, "The First Snow" woodcut.

Page 3, "A Familiar Landmark" woodcut.

Page 6, photograph, "Four Little Country Girls."

Chapter Two headpiece, page 11, photograph of Benjamin and Cynthia Dungan.

Page 36, photographs of Ida Dungan Beloof and Julia Kimberlin Hall.

Page 37, photographs of Mamie O. Dungan and C. O. Dungan.

Page 54, photographs of Horace and Marjorie Dungan.

Chapter Three headpiece, page 52, "Threshing" woodcut.

Chapter Four headpiece, page 71, "District School" woodcut.

Chapter Five headpiece, page 87, "Country Church" woodcut.

Page 92, "Lonely Farmhouse" woodcut.

Chapter Six headpiece, photograph of Mamie Dungan and her four daughters: Irene, Hildred, Idylene and Avis.

Page 137, "Sunlight Through the Trees" woodcut.

Chapter Seven headpiece, photograph of Harry G. Carlson.

Preface

Reminiscence has always been the besetting vice of old age. Nothing repels the young more strongly than a sentence beginning, "Now when I was young —" I know. Didn't I let my grandparents die without communicating to me what it was like to grow up before the Civil War? They tried, poor dears, but their audience wouldn't sit still.

And so, what possible reason can there be for me to suppose that the life and doings of an obscure housewife can be of interest to people outside her immediate circle? Particularly, if her life undoubtedly reeks of middle class values and Middle Western folklore? If she pleads that the social historians regularly announce that more changes have occurred in her lifetime than in the previous millenium, she must concede that nobody exactly falls over himself to learn about the days when the internal combustion engine was very young.

The sad fact seems to be that people read accounts of the infancy of the twentieth century with indulgent smiles and pass quickly on to more important pages. Most people are too fully engaged in the struggles of the present to care much about what happened to a child confronting a new century in the hinterlands of Southern Kansas.

Furthermore, most obscure dabblers in autobiography can at least claim participation in some national adventure. The story of a literate cowhand or a foot soldier in a famous campaign is likely to find appreciative readers. I can claim no such experience. What then entitles me to suppose that what happened to me is worth setting down on paper?

Only this: I survived the changes — and applaud most of them.

I lived through the tag-ends of the frontier with its passionate individualism to a time when a guaranteed minimum income is being considered; from a time when hard work and getting ahead were the great virtues, through the Lost and the Beat Generations to the Hippies, and on to the New Left and subsistence agricultural communes, and eventually to the

*Symbionese Liberation Front; through the upheavals fathered
by Marx and Freud to an age when the descendants of Einstein have thrust us into Space and given us the power to
destroy our species; through the Great Depression and the
wars Hot and Cold; from an isolated rural neighborhood to a
metropolitan area covering eight counties and no telling how
many municipalities; from a time when communication was
face to face or handwritten to a time when the funeral of a
European statesman or the misery of Vietnamese peasants
comes instantly into the living room. And as if these changes
which I myself have witnessed were not enough, I am, because I often lived with my grandparents, a bridge between a
generation of post-Civil War prairie pioneers who had precious few choices and had to make-do with bitter scarcities and
my grandchildren's generation, half-smothered in the choices
afforded by the Throw-away Society.*

*Through it all I had the animal wit to roll with the changes
instead of setting my heels and resisting.*

*As a result I have reached an old age which I greatly enjoy,
although my childhood and youth had all the ingredients
for a first-class neurosis.*

*At the same time I am impressed with how few of my con-
temporaries maintain affection for life. They cling to it, but
they do not like what they see it becoming. Almost none of
them continues to be a whole-hearted member of the present. I
feel that I have not only survived the changes but have been
and still am a participant in the unfolding drama. For that
reason the story may be worth writing.*

*If so, how shall I write it? There is a severe limit to what
one remembers. In the long wash of the years, childhood and
youth come to be a vague flatland, broken by an occasional
peak of dramatic or catastrophic event or illumined by a
flash of some purely personal happening. Having been, after a
fashion, a writer of stories, I could fill in and plump out
between the peaks with imagined details. Or as a practiced
student it would be easy to fill in and plump out through
research.*

*To write only of what I remember or was told first-hand
will be limiting, but it is the way I have chosen.*

Small World, Long Gone

The Child

I keep my first picture hanging on my bedroom wall so as to remind me: this is how you began. The photography is not much — an old-fashioned "enlargement" some itinerant salesman probably talked my parents into buying with money needed for many other things. But there she is (I cannot say "I" because I can feel no connection with the framed tot on the wall) looking out at the incoming twentieth century with somewhat slanted eyes. Her hair, I know from the strand Mother kept for me, was the color of newly threshed oat straw. Her face was round and cherubic, the button nose softly infantile. Only in the smile, the left corner rising slightly, is there hint of the questing and uncertainty which have plagued me throughout life.

I do not know how old she was that day when my parents set her down before a cumbersome old camera and a man put his head under a heavy black cloth. But the wary half-smile announces that she has already passed from what some psychologists call "the primal we" of union with the mother. That smile belongs to someone who already feels I-and-they and views her surroundings, including "them," with a certain estrangement. So she is at least two years old. Already she has several times been taken from her mother to a grandmother's care, the first time when she was only four months old and the mother had typhoid fever.

By the time she is four she will have become a "reader," addicted for life to print. Always she will read whatever her astigmatic eyes light upon and be on the prowl for pages which may illumine the riddles of both her surroundings and her own secretive self. And very early she will learn that among the surest smoke screens to be thrown up around the inner life to which she admits no one are a ready laugh and a light tongue. By the time she is ten she will know in her bones that surface conformity will fend off invaders nosing into the areas where all "they" are intruders. The lifted corner on the baby lips is an omen of the apartness which she will be a good many years in even beginning to overcome.

The world she looks out upon was tiny, though of course it seemed enormous to her. It contained perhaps a hundred people, a fifth of whom were relatives. She has not yet seen, and will not for several years, a Negro, a Jew, or a first generation immigrant. Only the presence of one Catholic family kept her neighborhood from being pure WASP — and that family seemed hardly to belong because its head not only "drank" and swore torridly but worked in his fields on Sunday afternoons after going to early Mass.

The time was the dying nineteenth century, the place a stock farm in the Flint Hills of Southern Kansas. For the non-Kansans who never heard of the Flint Hills, let me explain that they are a range perhaps fifty miles wide and 100 miles inside the Eastern border, reaching north and south across the state clear down into Oklahoma. As hills they aren't much, just long flat or round-topped uprisings studded with rocky outcroppings, interruped by creeks and even a few small rivers. Along these creeks grew trees and appeared the "bottom land" prized by farmers the world over. But by and large the Flints were cattle country, murder on plows, but growing a nutritious grass called "blue-stem" on which cattle throve and yearlings waxed fat. Cattle country it was, and unlucky the farmer without the gumption to recognize it as such. My father knew the Hills for what they were. He had smallish, bottom-land fields where grain crops were grown, but nearly all the income that came his way came walking on four feet.

Nothing sets that childhood home of mine in the Flint Hills more sharply apart from today than its mileages.

Twenty-five or so miles to the South is Indian Territory, not yet Oklahoma, but the child will have seen New York before she crosses the border into the Sooner state. Her parents never crossed it. Twenty miles to the South and East is the county seat, where her father must go several times a year. At such times he rises very early and is in his buggy by five in the morning. A good driving team could cover the distance in four hours, but he never felt justified in keeping such a team, though he never put the heavy-footed plow-horses and brood mares on the road. When his errands at the courthouse and the Ackarman Hardware and Mother's commissions at the dry goods store are finished, he will start home. He will not arrive until well after dark.

But distances of twenty and twenty-five miles are completely beyond the child's imagining. Come closer. Two  miles to the west are her paternal grandparents, two miles east the end of the neighborhood. Two and a quarter miles south are the real landmarks, Belknap church and school. Together the two white frame buildings house nearly all the neighborhood activities. Externally they are as alike as bottles on an assembly line. Of about the same dimensions, both are heated by corpulent coal-eaters unadorned by isinglass or polish. Both are lighted by bare windows. Both are enclosed by barbed wire fences to restrain cattle standing knee deep in blue stem.

Just inside the back fences stood identical little unpainted buildings whose presence everybody modestly ignored until

[3]

time of need. Some circumstance already lost in the mists of time has prompted the first settlers to affix to school yard rather than churchyard the awe-inspiring place where the child was taken when death struck in the neighborhood.

In these days church-going was adventure. First there was the exciting scrabble to get all the little girls into their Sunday clothes. Then we must be arranged in the "spring wagon," three of us in the back seat, the fourth between Father and Mother. Then we moved down our lane to join a somewhat larger road, then through the sultry yellow dust of summer or the stinging cold of winter for a full mile. It was undoubtedly the longest mile in Kansas, a state whose miles are noted for their length. Nothing but hedgerows and cornfields in that mile, its only landmark an occasional culvert. The second was better, for it provided three houses with a fourth easily visible though some distance back from the road. Around so many farmsteads it was practically guaranteed there would be something worth looking at, even if only a farm boy pursuing a long-legged fryer for the Sunday skillet. And finally we round another corner and another culvert and Father is tying the horses at the hitching rack. It has been a ride of body and soul-testing length, under cloud of two mandates: Mother's "Keep yourself clean," and Father's, "No quarreling back there."

But that ride is nothing compared to another. Seven miles to the north is "town." On a recent flight from Amsterdam seven miles were less than a minute, not long enough for me to repair a make-up. For astronauts it is hardly the flick of an eyelash. But *then*! How does one convey the enormity of seven miles to a child sitting beside her father in a wagon or her mother in a buggy? It was tedious, wearisome, hope deferred interminably, anticipation prolonged to the point of agony. It was *forever*.

First we went across the creek and alongside one of our woodlots, then past the cramped, unpainted homes of three neighbors. From one house to the next the wait for something to happen was long but it could be endured. But there followed a mile of nothing except cattle grazing on the low Flint Hills and perhaps, if we were lucky, an idiot cottontail hopping lazily ahead of us.

[4]

Once in a very blue moon there was real excitement, when in the distance a strange object came toward us in a cloud of dust. This object, looking much like a buggy but wondrously without horses, wasn't owned, we knew, by any one in the vicinity of Moline — not even the doctor or the banker. On sighting the visitor from outer space, Father hastily drove the team off the road. Then he sprang to their heads, caught their bridles firmly and began to talk to them in a tone calculated to soothe their nervous systems. As the object came alongside, the team lunged and reared. I have long wished that some one could explain the rapidity with which Dobbin adjusted to the new contraptions when the very early ones so terrified him. In a few years he paid them much less heed than the flies on his rump.

But such marvelous confrontations occurred rarely, at first perhaps only once or twice in a year. The Flint Hills were not designed by their Creator for quick adoption of the gasoline engine. During a good two-thirds of the year the roads were no more than a pair of ruts or a giant frozen crater or a thick pad of yellow dust masking knife-sharp outcroppings of limestone. Only the rarest of trips was enlivened by sight of a stranger driving a loud-thumping, vile-smelling ancestor of today's cars. On nearly all trips we simply plodded along.

From afar Old Boston would loom, a schoolhouse where Father once taught and my sister would some day teach. Eventually, *very* eventually, we came up beside it and I was able hungrily to note anything worth noting. Up and down more hills we crept, jouncing over stones, rolling over hollow-sounding wooden bridges. More miles dragged by, when it seemed that time would never end. And finally we were on the last long hill, at the bottom of which was a straggle of box-like buildings, a little town which had scarcely changed from its frontier days.

At long last we were across the railroad track and moving past the red station where the townspeople were said to gather on Sunday afternoons to see the West-bound come in. (The child would have to wait until she was going away to school before she had first-hand knowledge of this Lord's Day social practice.) At length we passed the Palace Hotel with

[5]

Four Little Country Girls — Irene, Hildred, Avis and Idylene

its long porch and many chairs for the accommodation of cigar-chewing travelling men, whose stares would later give her a strange but not wholly unpleasant feeling. A stop at the creamery to put out the heavy can. Then past the bank, where Father might later go to pay off a note or make another in order to feed out yet another lot of cattle. And the millinery store, where if Mother was along, she would manage to go and to look, though seldom to buy. Then the post-office where we would pick up our mail, the rural route not yet being in existence. And at last, oh at last, we were halfway up unpaved Main Street with its false fronts and brick sidewalks. Father hitched the horses in front of the Moline Mercantile, enchanted place, where perhaps calico for a new dress and certainly lemon and peppermint stick candy would be purchased.

The Moline Mercantile of any rural child of seventy years ago probably differed only slightly from that of other such children. Because mine burned down years ago, I have no notion of how large it would be in my adult eyes. But then it was *huge* — and somehow it made me feel big and important because the wife of the owner had gone to Normal with Mother, and if she chanced to be in the store they fell into each other's arms. To think that my mother knew the most important woman in town!

Groceries occupied one side of one aisle, with the usual sugar barrel and cracker boxes, sumptuous smelling Longhorn and fragrant dill pickles. Housewares took up the other side of the aisle. Yard goods and shoes and ready-to-wear were packed into the other two aisles. High above all, in the center of the store, the cashier sat regally pulling money out of the small boxes zooming up to her and speeding back the change. (She never sent back any money for us, for our bills were always charged until the next shipment of cattle or hogs went to Kansas City.) Back of the store were the outhouses. Naturally, the child never saw the inside of one of them, but the walls of the other were decorated with certain pencilled words and proverbs that she puzzled over every time her mother or grandmother procured the key on its long paddle and led her "out back."

By comparison to the long-drawn agony of the ride into town, homegoing was easy and quick, mercifully passed in a heavy slumber.

A child's world, restricted and restricting? Yes. But it was also the world of most adults in the neighborhood. Hardly anyone under forty had been farther than the county seat. In general, only "old settlers" and Civil War veterans, both groups now much thinned out, had first-hand knowledge of the outer world. Of course, whoever had managed to get as far as eighth-grade geography knew that there were such places as Brazil and China, but the place-names meant little more than colors on a map representing countries off somewhere in space, of no concern to Belknapers. Cuba was real because a young man had recently been there and so was now able to join the GAR veterans on Memorial Day.

Nor was the child's earth all that occupied very limited space. The universe itself was small. One of my earliest memories is of running up and down the dooryard with a broom pointed upward. When some one asked my child-self what she was doing, she replied innocently that she was trying to sweep down a star. The memory has stayed with me because the resulting laughter let the child know that she had been ridiculous — and even then she was not one to be ridiculous if she could help it. For the same reason I remember the evening when the moon seemed to rest on the ridgepole of the house and a ladder had been left against the eaves. When the child was hustled down by horrified adults, she threw them off the trail by claiming that she liked to climb ladders. But in her heart she remained convinced, because she had *seen* it, that the wonderful shining ball had been there on the roof peak. (The thought just now occurs, did this early experience account for my life-long skittishness about heights?)

While of course no adult in the neighborhood had so childish a notion of the limits of space, most of them probably did share in other aspects of the limitation. For instance, we all believed that heaven was somewhere out of sight "up there." And if we were church people we knew that God sat somewhere "up there" and that if we were good, we would some day go to dwell with Him. If any of us had known German and chanced upon Schiller's ecstatic *Uber'n Sternenzeit, Muss ein leiber Vater wohnen,* we would have accepted it quite literally.

If adults did not share the child's belief that the twinkles of the stars were caused by people walking on the floor of a gloriously lighted heaven, it was only because they lacked the fantasy-power of a child. For them, too, the universe was strictly limited. If some one had told them that the flaxen-haired child would live to a time when a man-made star plowing through space at around 100,000 miles an hour would require many months to pass beside Jupiter, the idea would have seemed to them the bubbling of an overtaxed mind.

If space was severely restricted, consider how cramped was time. In the margin of the Bible presented to the child on her tenth birthday, the opening line, "In the beginning God created —" carries a marginal note: "4004 B.C." Even at age ten that second 4 fascinated her. How, she wondered, could any one be so sure of it?" But the adults in her world assured her that there were learned students of the Bible who had computed Hebrew history so carefully that they knew the very year when God undertook His great task. A half-century after its publication the ferment touched off by *The Origin of the Species* had not arrived in Belknap. To have told my grandparents or even my parents that life had been on earth for at least two billion years would have been a waste of breath. They *knew* that the earth had been "without form and void" less than six thousand years ago. Who could have predicted that the child's son would be a student of the evolution of galaxies?

I can drive from my home back to that locale, but I would not find the neighborhood, though some of my contemporaries are still there. Time has happened to it as to me. Time — two great wars, gasoline engines, television antennae, high school diplomas and the agricultural revolution have shaken it out of its snug protections.

postscriptum, 1975

As I look back from my present sense of being involved in all things human, I can scarcely believe the isolation of my childhood. But though we could not know it then, that isolation was already under attack. The Rural Free Delivery Act was passed by Congress in 1896, the year that I was born. As usual, the ensuing change did not reach us immediately. But I can vaguely remember when Father installed a metal tube on a post on the "main road," a good city block from our house. It was not nearly as big as the rural boxes needed to accommodate all of today's periodicals and junk mail, but it was big enough. In it, six days a week, a man in a dusty or mud-speckled buggy deposited a *Topeka Daily Capital.* The *Youth's Companion* came for the young and, once a month, the *Delineator* for Mother. From the country seat came the *Sedan Times-Star.* Sometimes there was even a letter. No

[9]

wonder "getting the mail" was a chore so dearly prized that I was often too early and hid under the bridge until the clatter of wheels overhead, the stop of the buggy and then the roll of wheels told me that our civil servant was gone. There might not be much in the box, but there was always the *Daily Capital* with the Katzenjammer Kids and Mutt and Jeff. I could not then dream that one day I would carry a good part of the daily deposit unopened to the waste basket.

The second isolation-breaker was, of course, the telephone. Alexander Graham Bell got his patent in 1876, but it was after 1900 before a party line was established among us, one for the whole neighborhood. In the beginning installing telephone lines was a local, cooperative effort. The neighbor men cut, trimmed, and installed their own gnarled and quirky Osage Orange posts. These were rarely as much as eight feet high and the lines often sagged to no more than four feet above the ground. But oh, the miracle of "ringing up" and talking with young friends who lived two or three *miles* away!

2

Typical of the era is this charming, posed photograph of grandparents, Benjamin and Cynthia Dungan

The Family

In mid-August of 1895 the county seat newspaper noted that Cyrus O. Dungan and Mary Alice Howard had recently taken out a marriage license. The item went unnoticed in the Belknap neighborhood, Grandmother D used to intone, because nobody recognized either party. It seems the groom detested the name of Cyrus and from the time he could assert himself had been known as "Ollie," while the bride had always been "Mamie Hall." To a listening child, who felt that Cyrus was a distinguished name and Ollie somehow unfitting for the big-boned six-footer who was her father, his choice was only another of the unfathomable ways of adults. But that her mother — her pretty, her light-and-swift-moving mother — should have had a secret name which she had to reveal in order to get married, that was romance itself.

When Ollie and Mamie went down to the courthouse on that hot August day, they carried with them, the Dungan and Grandstaff, the Howard and Kimberlin family strains. So far as I know, only the Dungans ever had anybody disposed to genealogical research, and that somebody became known to us much later and came from quite a different branch of the tree. Thanks to him and the thick book he got together, I know very much more about the Dungans than any of the other three families.

But even without The Book, as we have always called it, I would have known more about the Dungans, for they were the ones I had to deal with most often and most intimately. Mother had what was then known as a "weak constitution." She was not one of the storied females who can sail un-ravaged through four pregnancies in six years, particularly not when the three youngest little girls were subject to ear aches and sore throats in a day when an ear ache almost inevitably went to drum rupture and a sore throat to the long agony of tonsilitis. So I was always being packed off to a grandmother. And because Grandmother Hall was also frail, the usual caretaker was Grandmother D, undoubtedly the most unfrail woman in Kansas.

One of my very early memories is of snuggling under her worn plush cape while clutching the sketchy remains of a woolly toy whose identity I've long since forgotten. The strength of her thick warm body and the steady thump of her heart must have been more comforting than my "softy," for it is that strength I remember, along with the heavy, iron-bound wheels grinding against limestone ledges or lurching in the ruts if there had recently been rain. It would be years before I could fit the word "exiled" to my childish woe, and I would have children of my own before I understood that my harried young parents selected *me* for the exile because they were trying to protect Grandmother by turning over to her the child who was not only older but healthy.

Later, when it was time for school, I spent the winter with her, because she lived only a few rods from a school house, while my parents were two and a half miles away, too far for a six-year-old to undertake by foot or horse. Let no eyebrows be lifted at the reference to a horse. Thanks to the high pommel on our Western saddles and leather slips above the stirrups, I could by age six ride a darting cow pony so well that nobody worried unduly about my falling off. But small hands and feet could freeze in bad weather. Besides, the fourth child was very young and the ear aches and sore throats were still about. By this time the sense of exile had been tempered by the canny perception of the bonuses inherent in grandparental charge, with no competition from Little Sisters. Later, when I was thirteen and ready for high school and the Grandparents D had moved to a town fifty miles away, they got me again, this time for four winters. In the course of all this sojourning I got to know Dungans very well indeed.

Since Father and Mother were the oldest in their families, young uncles and aunts were growing up in both households to spoil me, laugh at my antics and boss me. There were, however, twice as many uncles and aunts in the Dungan clan, and I was their pet and long-eared pest more often.

The first American Dungans were brought by their mother and stepfather to Rhode Island in 1637 as children. According to The Book, their father, who was a younger son of a younger son of Sir John Dungan of Dublin, had died in London the year before, leaving a widow and four young children. The next year Frances Dungan married Jeremy Clarke, brother to a young Baptist minister who had recently been banished from the Massachusetts Bay Colony and who had joined Roger Williams in Rhode Island. Dungan had been Irish and Catholic, Frances was Anglican, the Clarkes were Baptist. Of all the dissenting groups of that dissenting period, the Baptists believed most deeply in religious freedom. So when Archbishop Laud intensified his campaign to make all dissent a crime, young Clarke picked up his new wife and ready-made family and made the long hard voyage to Rhode Island, there to become one of the Incorporators of Newport.

The Clarke children (Frances went on to have seven of them) mostly remained in Rhode Island to become governors, legislators and other people of importance. Even most of the Dungans seem to have stayed in the East and done well. But my ancestor became a Baptist minister and later got a grant of land in Bucks County from William Penn himself.

From the Reverend Thomas, born in London and dying in 1687, to my grandfather, born in Indiana in 1843, it was a

[13]

long hop. But the Reverend Thomas set the pattern in two ways: first, by moving from Rhode Island to New Jersey and then on to Pennsylvania; and second, by setting up the first Baptist church in the state. Generation after generation, his descendants went West, cutting down forests, turning prairie sod, and moving further West when things went awry, which they regularly did. In three or four generations they had become prime examples of that hardy, poverty-stricken, untrammeled, unlettered breed known as frontiersmen. Grandfather himself was born in Indiana, enlisted in the Union Army from Illinois, went on to Eastern Kansas at the War's end, later moved three times in Kansas, two of the times to newer neighborhoods. Not until my father's generation, when the frontier was gone did the line settle down to battle their fate wherever they happened to have been born. (Oddly enough, his was the only generation to do so. Beginning with mine, education made wanderers of us again.)

The second style-setting bequest from the Reverend Thomas was his religious fervor. Perhaps that and his uncompromising devotion to the truth as he saw it were reinforced by his marriage to Elizabeth Freeborn Weaver, daughter and granddaughter of men driven out of the Massachusetts theocracy, but I strongly doubt that his convictions needed any wifely reinforcement. Somewhere in the six generations which separated him from Grandfather, the Baptist faith became Methodist, but the fervor remained. By the time I knew him he was a lay or "local" preacher and often away from home holding or attending revival meetings. He organized the first "class" at Belknap and was the prime mover in building the church. From early middle age he sought "sanctification," a state in which Methodists of that era believed that one was beyond even the temptation to sin. At times he believed, or at least hoped, that he had attained his quest.

Again like his progenitor, he lost his father at an early age. But the Reverend Thomas had a mother and a decent, responsible stepfather. Grandfather's mother died when he was only four, and he was then turned over to one or another of his older brothers and sisters until he could shift for himself. Perhaps they did as well by him as they could in the harsh new Illinois neighborhoods, but they were often unkind to him and gave him less than six months' schooling.

When the Civil War broke out, he was just past eighteen. He and two of his brothers enlisted at once in an Illinois regiment formed at Springfield to serve under Grant. After chasing General Jeff Thompson through Missouri (on foot), the outfit went on to the bloody battles of Ft. Henry, Ft. Donelson, Shiloh, Pittsburg Landing, and the long, misery-soaked conquest of Vicksburg, in which a brother was killed. Grandfather was among those present in Springfield when the remnants of the regiment was mustered out in June, 1864. He was not able to re-enlist because a case of measles plus pneumonia contracted while in the service had left him with "bad lungs."

A few months after his discharge Benjamin Dungan married Cynthia Grandstaff, a year and a half older than he, and the daughter of Irish Presbyterian immigrants. It was not an auspicious match. The groom had *no* prospects: no money, no education, not even any health. His family experiences had been wretched and he had been looking death in the eye for three years. Moreover, he earnestly believed that a man should be absolute head of his household. No sensible young woman should have looked at him twice.

Cynthia was loaded with common sense, but she was also twenty-three and a half, an age then considered to be bumping the threshhold of hopeless old-maidhood, and husband material was being slaughtered on every Southern battlefield. She may even have felt romantic about him for a time. At any rate, although she had a good touch of the superbly healthy person's contempt for weakness and had begun to harbor the subversive new notion that women are as smart as men, she took him. And lived with him for forty-nine hard years.

Even at the beginning they must have been an odd-looking pair, for he was six-two and a redhaired blonde, while she never got much past five feet and had raven hair and bright dark eyes. From his years of marching he had learned to swing his long legs in an easy rhythm that took him over the ground faster than most farm horses could manage. He was a minor marvel in the neighborhood because if he had an errand to do five or six miles away, he was likely to take "shank's mare" rather than hitch up a team. In his later years he made little effort to adjust his steps to hers, with the result that she half trotted to keep up with him or lagged behind if it happened to be one of her "independent feeling" days.

From my earliest recollection her stout little figure was shaped like a keg, with wide-toed shoes pushing out from under long full skirts, and a round little head protruding from the top of the keg. Her gait was slow and rolling, not ungraceful but notable only because it could be maintained indefinitely. She hadn't a glimmer of style, but there was something so solid and dependable about her as to attract anybody in trouble.

For many years she was a staunch advocate of woman's suffrage on grounds that, first, she was every bit as smart as her husband and, second, that her daughters-in-law were a good deal smarter than their husbands. *Therefore,* she would deduce triumphantly, she and they had a right . . .

Her sons had various strong opinions on the matter, but since Grandfather's views of womankind were colored by much reading of St. Paul, he regarded the prospect of women meddling in politics as sheer disaster.

This argument raged from my earliest memory until the day when Kansas finally granted suffrage. Having seen in the evening paper that the legislature had capitulated, one of the men patted her on the shoulder and said, expecting her to rejoice, "Now you can come along with us to the polls." Her reply floored me. "I can, but I never will." Nor did she.

She had a way of seeing in people resemblances to animals. As sure as she came home from church saying the preacher had made her think of a donkey in the way he threw out his jaw and hee-hawed through his nose, I saw that she was right and thereafter sat in fascinated contemplation of the likeness. Or if she said a neighbor looked like a rat ready to jump I could never afterwards look into his beady eyes without a slight shudder. Or if a woman brought to childbed too often got to looking like "a draggled-out mama-cat," she remained so for me. I even, God forgive me, began to see resemblances for myself.

Illogical she might be, but she was superwoman in one respect: I never heard her find fault with any of her daughters-in-law — and to a woman they were in her camp. This was a family where the women stuck together, except for the only daughter, who enjoyed men's talk, took on men's concern with politics and economics, and was always somewhat disdainful of feminine frivolity.

The basic difference between Benjamin and Cynthia was in temperament. Her parents had brought with them from Ulster a full freight of Calvinist impatience with error. She became a working Methodist, meaning that she was at times superintendent of some struggling little Sunday School and that she bedded and boarded not only the "presiding elders" on their quarterly rounds but the regular ministers when they needed a bed and fried chicken. But she always refused to be taken into formal membership. The optimistic, emotional ways of the sect never sat easily upon her. Eventually she learned not to argue about predestination, but it was a struggle.

When they married she set to work at once to teach him to read and succeeded so well, she always said drily, that somehow he always had an important book at hand just when the corn needed plowing. She herself never had much time for reading — She bore ten children, the last when she was forty-three — and raised seven of them. She cooked with a wood fire, scrubbed with lye soap, washed clothes on a board, raised her own poultry and grew her own vegetables, made the family's soap and clothing, even to the men's overalls.

In the midst of these regular activities of a pioneer woman she early became a midwife. No matter how brutal a day's work she had done or how queasy she felt from something shaping up in her own womb, a knock on the door in the middle of the night meant jumping into her clothes, riding the horse the prospective father had led, ready for whatever lay ahead with the meager facilities available. I doubt if she ever received a dollar for her services. On the frontier nobody had money to pay for the good offices of a neighbor. Gratitude was expressed by meat at butchering time or some kind of reciprocal helping-hand in time of need.

Benjamin, on the other hand, was a frustrated intellectual, completely miscast as a pioneer farmer. With his wife's help at the beginning he learned not only to read but to spell

[17]

(though he never learned not to put an extra "t" in "city") and to write a good hand. He worked his way through a stray copy of Euclid and taught himself how to survey. He read Dickens and the other British novelists whenever he could lay hands of them. With his daughter he read *Paradise Lost* aloud until they knew good-sized chunks of it by heart. Once he was engrossed in a book, it was next to impossible for him to tear himself loose from it. One of the stories he liked to tell on himself (Cynthia never found it funny) was of being unable to put down *Oliver Twist*. He read all night by his kerosene lamp, and when he had finished, was so ashamed of his weakness that he used the book to light the breakfast fire.

*   *   *

The Homestead Act of 1860, granting 160 acres of land to any head of a family who would live on them for five years, had been amended in 1862 to allow each year of military service to count as one of the prescribed five. Grandfather would therefore need only two years of residence in order to "prove up on a claim." The nearest open land was in Kansas, which was higher and drier than Illinois and presumably better for bad lungs. So to Kansas he went as his ancestors had gone from England to Rhode Island, to New Jersey, to Eastern then Western Pennsylvania, to Ohio, to Kentucky, to Indiana, to Illinois. One of his brothers went to Nebraska after the War, another to Oklahoma, and another to South Dakota. It was in the blood!

But the plan had to wait a bit. The War was still on, and Missouri's Little Dixie was a hornet's nest of guerillas, not a salubrious place for travelers in a covered wagon. Besides, even for homesteading a man had to have a little capital: a team, a wagon, a few basic tools, some kind of bed and stove, and at least a modicum of cash. Even after the long trip from Illinois began, it was halted for a time on the banks of the Mississippi by the birth and death of a premature baby. Malaria also struck, so that the young movers were less than half alive by the day in 1866 when they took up their "claim" in the eastern tier of Kansas counties.

Perhaps their lot as pioneers was no grimmer than most, but it was grim enough. During the first winter they almost starved on a diet of corn meal and molasses and whatever game Grandfather could knock over without benefit of ammunition, which required money. Cynthia, pregnant with my father, suffered a recurrent nightmare in which she watched her mother throw away white bread in spite of her daughter's frantic pleas. (This oft-told dream was one of my firmest bridges back to pioneer life, which by my time had begun to be romanticized by people who hadn't been through it.)

Toward the first spring the new neighborhood decided that some kind of school must be held. Two months was all that could be financed and since Grandmother was the person best qualified to deal with the Three R's, she got the job of teaching, though my father was to be born in April. Each morning she and Grandfather carried the bed, table and "safe" (cupboard) outside the cabin and placed some hand-hewn planks across stools to serve as seats. Then each evening the "benches" went out and the furniture came back in. For the two month term the salary was exactly thirty dollars, enough to buy, oh heavenly joy, a creature which would furnish not only milk but calves to grow into meat.

But according to the family annals (all the Dungans loved to spin out a good yarn, roaring with laughter as they talked) the cow turned out to be a most unruly beast. She wouldn't lead and when they tried taking off the rope she bolted across the prairie. The owners had pulled and pushed until their tempers frayed. They stormed after her in chase until they were breathless. That is, Benjamin did. Cynthia was too close to childbed to do much chasing. When he finally got the rope back around the creature's neck, it refused to budge.

At last in her Irish wrath Grandmother is said to have screamed, "Kill her, Ben, kill her!' Grandfather, at the end of *his* emotional tether, picked up a stick and gave the wretched animal a good clout over the head. To their horror she dropped instantly, the deadest looking cow they ever saw. Whereupon Cynthia sank to the ground and began to keen, "Oh, Ben dear, you've killed our cow, you've killed our cow." Bossy, however, was only stunned and soon got up and was forever after, so the Dungans claimed, amenable to rope and prod.

Another bridge back to the early days was the story of

Grandfather's getting a winter job away from the farm, working on the railroad, perhaps. He walked four miles each morning and evening to put in a twelve-hour day for the sum of one dollar — and was deeply grateful for a chance at those exceptionally good wages. On those long daily walks he usually carried a gun, hoping to pot a rabbit or prairie chicken.

Like all early Kansans, the Dungans had their tale of the fabled grasshopper invasion in 1874. As the young settlers rushed out to try to save something from the voracious swarms, they noticed that their turkey gobbler was smartly snapping up an unwonted feast. As the day passed and the fields and pastures became bare, the sorrowing couple walked back to their cabin over ground literally crawling with insects. In both minds was black worry over survival through the next winter. Just as they got back into the yard, they saw something which provoked a smile even then and later convulsed many a grandchild. The gobbler was walking about in a tipsy daze, completely indifferent to the still beckoning feast. From his mouth hung one horny little leg. He had done his level best to fight off the plague but hadn't been able to get his last hopper completely down.

Kaw Indians were still around, reasonably friendly but utterly poverty-stricken. When one of them rode into a settler's yard and asked for food, it was not considered politic to refuse. Sometimes the food requested was named Fido. If so, a child might wail his head off but Fido departed with the Indian. Or so Grandmother said, with the dark air of a woman who was maybe not too unhappy to be rid of an extra pup.

Once in an unusually confidential mood, she told me of her experience when one of her boys wet the bed until a late age. "He was such a sleepy-head the clap of doom wouldn't wake him. I tried everything anybody ever told me, but every blessed morning his bed was soaking and every blessed morning I had to wash it or in a few days the smell would blow you straight out of the house. One day a fine idea came into my head. I told him I had heard of a sure cure — if the young one drank a glass of milk that a mouse had been drowned in, he would never again fail to wake. Then I handed him a glass of milk. He begged and he pled, but I made him down it and I made him keep it down. Sure, and he could always wake up after that."

"*Had* you drowned a mouse in the milk?" I asked in near total shock.

"Of course not," she said with a snap of her black eyes. "But don't you go thinking things. I didn't actually tell him I had. I just told him I had heard it was a sure cure. I was so pesty tired of all that washing I had to do something."

But virtuous as she sounded, I would bet money that she never told her husband of the incident.

The years were hard, but Cynthia Grandstaff Dungan found a life in them. In body and spirit she was built, I almost said *created,* for the frontier. No woman in any of the three new neighborhoods where she lived was more needed and respected. Her role as a midwife guaranteed that.

One of her earlier deliveries taught her what she held to be a basic lesson. The patient had never been able to bear a live baby. It was therefore with a real sense of triumph that Grandmother gave the newcomer the customary spank and heard a lusty yell. She handed the baby over to its jubilant father and turned to finish caring for the mother. When she could get back to the baby, it was dead. The father had given it two teaspoonsful of whisky as a medication for tuning up the newborn's system. After that she laid down a cast iron law: NO WHISKY. And whenever anybody told her that whisky has its place, her standard retort was, "Sure it does, and that place is in hell." Off hand, I can't think of any other subject on which she and her husband saw so exactly eye to eye.

On another occasion she was attending a woman in hard labor with her first child and, of course, no pain-relievers of any sort. The husband was a tenderhearted young fellow devastated by her suffering. When the wife in her torment suddenly railed at him, "See what you did to me, just see what you did," he burst into tears and fled. "Sure, now," Grandmother sternly admonished, "we all know there were two people in that bed."

Eventually babies began to be delivered by doctors and the midwifing role faded out. Even then, however, Grandmother still got occasional emergency calls when it was obvious that some baby was in too much of a tearing hurry to wait for a man to ride miles to fetch a doctor. The fact of her presence in the neighborhood must have given many a swollen farm wife a sense of security.

The midwife role disappeared, but another went on. In a different time and place she would have been a gifted nurse. In pioneer neighborhoods where there were no trained nurses (Clara Barton was born only twenty years before Grandmother) families took care of their own illnesses. But when the Big Killers appeared everybody, including the doctor, felt easier if Mother Dungan was on the scene. Pneumonia, typhoid, diphtheria, cholera morbus, scarlet fever — she fought them all with at least as much success as came to the professionals of the era. And if she lost her fight, she washed and laid out the dead and stayed to shelter the bereaved with her strength and practical good sense.

Benjamin, who was no farmer at all, had his role and an important one. Through lean years and good and through all the ructions attendant on the rearing of six sons, Grandfather held on the course marked out by pioneer Methodism. He "read a chapter" after every breakfast and knelt by his chair to pray. His code of morals was rooted in the Methodist Discipline: it was wicked (and he meant *wicked*) to drink, smoke, dance, or play cards. He himself did not even drink coffee, his morning eye-opener being a cup of hot water liberally laced with sugar and cream. He thrashed sons so careless as to let him hear them swear. He never allowed a team in the field or a postponable chore on Sunday.

But he did not assume that obedience to all these "thou shalt nots" was sufficient. In a long life well peopled with Methodists I have never known one who took more seriously the Methodist belief in the possibility of perfection. On the frontier such a man was certain to be the religious leader of the community. The poker-playing, whisky-nipping men around him undoubtedly had much fun over his peculiar notions. But during spells of illness, when they perhaps fell to wondering about the possibility that the smoking pit might actually exist, they must have been glad to have so convinced a man in their midst, no matter how daftly he ran on about sanctification.

[22]

Since both grandparents believed passionately in education, they were leaders in their rural school districts. Somehow they saw to it that their children went to school on time and with enough food in their bellies and "dinner buckets" to let them learn. Their sons were not taken out of the five- or six-month term which was then standard. Four of them and their sister taught school at least for a time. The two youngest sons even got college degrees. Such a family was always important in frontier school districts.

But in the fourth neighborhood, a town of 10,000 where the younger children went to a Methodist "academy" and on to a struggling little college, Benjamin and Cynthia were misfits — of no consequence in the community, accorded no respect and even regarded as somewhat comic. Doctors and trained nurses, hospitals and undertakers were available. And a college-educated preacher left to Grandfather only a front seat, from which to embarrass me and amuse my contemporaries by giving forth an occasional "amen" when the man in the pulpit was especially apt.

Thinking back on the Dungan uncles and aunt, I am tempted to believe that I must have made them up. Surely such a driving, noisy, disputatious, haranguing, quick-raging crew could have existed only in a child's imagination. The trouble with this thesis is that I knew them when I was fully adult and they were middle-aged. They mellowed and quieted, but only somewhat.

The parents set the pattern, of course. Once, years after Grandmother's death, I wrote a jingle which I called "Memory" but which describes the subject matter of their long debate:

> Grandad was six-two and a redhead,
> Grandmom was five-none and Ulster bred;
> She was an ardent Democrat,
> He was for his General Grant;
> She talked darkly of predestination,
> He was Methodist who aimed at sanctification.
> When the children came, he feared to spare the rod,
> She declared she could manage with a nod.
> Grandad knew by chapter and verse
> That women voting would be a curse,
> It made her boil to think noodles like Jasper Bott

[23]

Could vote and she could not.
Every night she flounced off to bed while he sat
    conning a book,
Every dawn she bounced him out of bed by some sly
    hook or crafty crook.
When she was gone, he proudly and often averred,
"We lived together forty years and never spoke
    a cross word."

Perhaps the words were never cross, but many of them were certainly *warm*.

Other interminable discussions went on between Grandfather and Grandmother's brother Elisha, who had gone with Sherman to the sea. The two old soldiers could work up a temper any day disputing the military merits of their generals. But somehow the argument nearly always shifted to theology, and instead of Grant and Sherman being wheeled up against each other, it would be text and counter text. In the first stirrings of skepticism, the bored child used to wonder if some of the disputants' assiduous Bible-study were not a search for new ammunition.

The one argument which never bored her concerned what the Presbyterian called "predestination" and the Methodist insisted was "infant damnation." Could it be, she wondered, that a baby came into the world so cursed by Adam's sin that unless it lived to grow up and find salvation it was doomed to eternal death in the fires of hell? In view of the number of infants making their appearance in the child's vicinity this was a good subject for speculation. But since it also affected her own situation, it was one argument where she rooted wholeheartedly for her grandfather.

The parents may have set the pattern, but the daughter and six sons took to it like larks to wing. It was a family which loved, really *loved,* to marshal facts and figures in support of opposing views. Anything would do for a subject: religion, ethics, woman's suffrage, the grip of the "money power," Sockless Jerry's latest doing, the cause of panics, the veracity of a neighbor — any subject whatever, provided only that it was something a body could get his teeth into and shake until its bones rattled.

Of all topics their favorite was politics. Only a few years

had elapsed since Byran's "cross of gold" speech and Mary Ellen Lease's fiery trek up and down Kansas advising farmers to raise less corn and more hell. Proponents of woman's suffrage were getting themselves arrested. Theodore Roosevelt was beginning to shake his big stick and to threaten to bust the trusts. (How the arguments raged later during the presidential campaign of 1912 when Father was Old Guard, Uncle Frank a Bull Mooser, and Aunt Ida a newly converted Socialist!

Grandmother was as illogical as the next female and was therefore regularly shoved aside by her husband and offspring, all of whom believed mightily in themselves as logicians, but she could never bring herself to stay out of the arguments which swirled about her until sometimes the very ceiling seemed to quiver and mayhem loomed as the only likely outcome. These were no occasions for women to be abroad, except the black-eyed daughter of the house, who could hold her own and better, but Grandmother was never able to resist them.

Why, I used to wonder from the sidelines, *did they have to get so excited?* In the early years the question was asked in curiosity. Later, as I touched adolescence, in contempt. Early and late, it was asked by a simon-pure outsider.

Not until much later did I realize my luck in growing up among the voluble, dogmatic, contentious Dungans. They all had bone-deep integrity. Not one of them was a liar or a cheat. Not one of them would ever refuse to lend a hand to a neighbor in trouble, and the definition of "neighbor" was broad. Because they had strong convictions about many things and few doubts about anything, one always knew where they were. A child could do much worse than grow up among them, even as an outsider.

*   *   *

I wish I knew more about "the other side of the house." Mother's father was a Civil War Veteran named Howard. He came to Kansas from Indiana and had fought on the Union side. Mother always said her father was descended from the Virginia Howards, but since he died before she was born and she had no direct contact with his family, I do not know

[25]

how she could have been sure. Perhaps he told her mother during the brief marriage. A faded old tintype of him in his soldier's uniform shows him to have been a handsome young man with well-chiselled features and a serious countenance.

From the time I was old enough to make any observations, I understood that this grandmother was very different from the other. Both were about five feet tall, but there the resemblance ended. Where one had black hair and strong, heavy bones, the other was a delicately built blonde with tiny hands and feet and a neat little figure that time and four children failed to thicken.

She always fascinated me. Her hair was regularly put up on papers, and her interest in clothes never flagged even though, caught in the dry pinch of frontier life, the poor darling had almost no money to spend on them. Her flowered "bonnet," her black lace mitts, her silk "reticule," the embroidery and fine tucks on her petticoats, the handmade lace on the white apron in which she presided over a company dinner, the "ear bobs" in her pierced lobes — all charmed me and set this grandmother apart from the other women in the neighborhood. Neither Mother nor I was resentful when Father sometimes said, handing the three of us into the carriage, "Three generations, and the older the prettier." Or at least I wasn't. I knew he was merely stating fact.

Her story is both romantic and pathetic. She was never made for pioneering. She was born into comfortable circumstances in Kentucky and reared to be cherished by a comfortably situated man. Her parents died when she was young, leaving her to the guardianship of an older brother. Kentucky families and neighborhoods were divided in their allegiances, but I think the Kimberlins must have been Union sympathizers because Grandmother never exhibited a trace of the Southern sorrow over the "lost cause." This indifference may have meant only that she was too young for the War to have affected her, but in the families concerned with the Confederacy, very small children were caught up in the family grief. Furthermore, if she had felt about Union soldiers as hosts of Southern girls did, she could hardly have married one as casually as she did.

The pivotal fact in Juliet Kimberlin's early life was not

the War but asthma, in those days a curse from which the only known relief was a lucky change of climate. Doctors agreed that while not every change helped, a drier atmosphere sometimes seemed to help. Many child asthmatics either died or were invalided. Juliet escaped those fates, but she was crippled and inconvenienced.

In early 1871 several of the lesser families from her neighborhood were going out to settle in Southern Kansas. Every schoolchild knew that Kansas was part of the Great American Desert and therefore might be good for asthma. The immediate spur to action was the fact that eighteen-year-old Juliet's best beau had just been, to quote my mother, "discovered in a compromising situation" with another girl. Juliet was hurt and furious, a scorned woman right down to her little boot tips. And Kansas just might be good for her asthma. So she talked a young couple into taking her with them in their covered wagon. Her brother stormed, but short of calling the sheriff there wasn't much he could do. He ended by giving her enough money to make the trip plus a stern injunction to come home if her asthma didn't improve. The beau implored forgiveness and later, when he thought she had had time to cool down, followed her and besought her to marry him. The resoluteness of her refusal was no doubt partly owing to the appearance, somewhere along the plodding journey, of William Howard.

His fate was probably sealed at first sight, for almost every man who set eyes on her seems to have felt an urge to take care of her. And one can understand how this most unlikely passenger in an emigrant's wagon must have appealed to him. And she? She never talked to me about it, but she was very angry, and good-looking young Howard was at hand. So they were married, probably somewhere in Western Missouri. Why they didn't turn back to Indiana or Kentucky I never knew, but perhaps it was no more than natural that having come so far they should want to see what Kansas might be like. Before they could even begin to find out, two things happened. Juliet became pregnant and the young husband contracted miliary tuberculosis, then known as "quick consumption." He was gone before Mother was born.

As if this were not enough disaster, the woman with whom

[27]

Juliet had come to Kansas died in childbirth. After Howard's death Juliet, now approaching her own delivery, had been living with the couple, so that she had to try to care for the premature baby. One of the most poignant frontier stories I know is of this widowed girl trying vainly to save her friend's baby while burdened with her own grief and anxiety. Because of the way she had been reared, she had no realistic knowledge of her body. No doubt full of old wives' tales, certainly fresh from her friend's death in childbirth, she was either too frightened or too "modest" to let a man know that labor had begun. She must have suffered emotional torture along with the usual pangs of parturition before the man finally discovered her plight and hurried to fetch a midwife.

I do not know for sure why she did not return to her brother when her infant was able to travel. (This is the sort of question children are rarely bright enough to ask when their elders are still about.) But probably it was because another man was eager to take care of her.

According to Mother, Ezra Hall was no hero, having spent the War in Canada evading the draft. He was twenty-two years older than Juliet, but good-looking, well-bred, fun-loving, and the owner of a spanking team of matched bays. For the time and place he was undoubtedly a bit of a sport — in Juliet's eyes a much better catch than the homely young German who also wanted to be her protector and who, as Mother once drily observed, went on to become the leading businessman in the County! So, when little Mamie was still a baby in arms and Juliet herself was nineteen she married her second husband.

The Hall family was very different from the book-reading, temperish Dungans. Where the Dungans read and argued, the Halls sang and joked. Everybody in it loved to sing. Charlie and Dency in particular had excellent untrained voices, and the whole family could harmonize. Charlie played both the fiddle and the harmonica by ear and could make a room jump when he turned in on *The Irish Washerwoman*. Grandmother had a true, though small voice and a good repertoire of folk and nursery songs, which in time descended to us along with a regular breakfast menu of ham and hot biscuits.

[28]

The Halls differed even more sharply from the Dungan household in another respect. Mr. Hall was never so poor or busy that he didn't manage to make some elderberry or wild blackberry wine to help liven up the evenings and the singing. One day when he was in town, he treated himself to something more potent and came home under its influence. As Mother told the story long afterward, he careened into the yard standing up in the buggy, flourishing his whip and singing joyously. Grandmother took one look, then flew out to him.

"Ezra," she said sternly, pulling up her whole sixty inches, "Ezra Hall, get out of that buggy at once and go to your bed before you make any more of a spectacle of yourself." The significant part of the story is that tipsy as he was, he broke off his song and went meekly to bed. It seems that over a period of time the frontier put iron into even such a woman as Juliet Kimberlin Howard Hall.

It was through this grandfather that at the age of four and a half I made my first acquaintance with death for human beings. (A farm child is, of course, surrounded by death of animals.) The peculiar hush that fell over grownups and the great black box that sat on four chairs in Grandmother's small "front room" were etched as deeply in memory as the thump of earth falling upon pine boards to the, "Dust thou art, to dust returnest." Ever afterwards there was shivery new meaning to the bedtime prayer which I, along with millions of other children, had been taught:

> Now I lay me down to sleep,
> I pray the Lord my soul to keep;
> If I should die before I wake
> I pray the Lord my soul to take.

My first separation from my mother, at the age of four months, was necessitated by her tussle with typhoid fever. It was a long separation, for the fever then took weeks to "run its course" and left its victim to a slow erratic convalescence. I think the early part of this first separation must have been spent with the Halls, because Grandmother D would have been chief nurse during that bad time. That I survived was counted a stroke of good fortune, for most babies weaned under such circumstances perished. Fortunately, there was a

[29]

cow which could be kept close and milk could be brought directly from udder to bottle.

Later sojourns with Halls came only at times when Cynthia was involved in some nursing stint or helping one of her daughters-in-law induct another newcomer into the rugged business of living.

I could not have been very old when I first realized that the two grandparental homes were very different and that it behooved me not to carry remarks from one to the other. When adolescent Dency Hall gave me a wicked imitation of adolescent Ida Dungan's hip-swinging gait, or when Ida gave me to understand that she considered Dency not only feather-brained but boy-crazy, my reaction was probably akin to that of a child of divorced parents: the shock of recognizing something I had not seen for myself; the pain of split loyalty; the freezing of lips over teeth in a resolve not to tattle. I had this series of responses over and over again. Especially I had them when one grandmother sniffed over the other's willingness to let her man do her thinking, or when the second confided that the first "makes things hard for herself. It doesn't pay a woman to be too strong." Young aunts were one thing, but mutually disdainful grandmothers were like God and Jesus belittling each other.

A child frequently passed back and forth between homes with such different values and a third with yet another set can hardly avoid learning that adults are not all-wise, which provides the soil for the growth of youthful skepticism. A bright child also learns to take advantage of the courting that inevitably comes his way, especially if one day he has a long serious illness. A child inclined for some reason to do himself mischief may arrive at the conclusion that he doesn't really belong to any of the three homes.

*　　*　　*

My parents were undoubtedly the most ambitious, hard-driving couple in the neighborhood, perhaps in the County. In their will to "get ahead" there was a kind of intensity that few young couples nowadays possess. One of my early memories is of a conversation between Mother at the ironing table and her father-in-law sitting beside it. What had been said before I tuned in probably had to do with the strain and overwork apparent to any one who crossed the threshhold.

"But, Daughter, you do not need to fret so," Grandfather was saying. "Our Lord said, 'Take ye no thought for the morrow. Sufficient unto the day is the evil thereof.'"

"We *have* to take thought," Mother interrupted with a fierce thrust of the flatiron. "We have four little girls to be educated and given a start in life."

"Consider the lilies, how they toil not, neither do they spin, yet I say unto you —" Grandfather began solemnly.

"Pooh," Mother snapped. "Lilies don't wear out shoes or get sick and have doctor bills."

With that I tuned out of the conversation, but it probably went on for a considerable time.

I never happened to overhear Father express himself on the subject of taking thought for the morrow, but it was obvious to his associates that his father might be content with high place in the Kingdom but he himself intended to have a place in the affairs of men as well as of God. *His* wife would not become a shapeless drudge, *his* children would go to college, he himself be respected by neighbor and banker.

He and Mother began to "go together" when she was sixteen and he twenty-two. I think it is literally true that neither of them was ever even slightly interested in any one else. Perhaps these ambitious young people recognized in each other a potential for growth greater than that of others in the neighborhood. Certainly the fact that she was so different from his mother and sister in her fine-boned slenderness and dancing blue eyes, her sharp interest in clothes, her wit and talent for mimicry must have appealed to him. And his drive and exceptional physique and protectiveness were quite different from what she encountered in her own family.

It was a long courtship and engagement, six years, because they both intended to "get a start" before assuming the risks of marriage. In those days marriage almost inevitably meant a quick start on family-making, and children were a handicap to an ambitious couple whose only capital was their own determined muscles and brains.

Why was it so important for them to get ahead that they could put off marriage in spite of being deeply in love? The answer, no doubt, lies in the special family situations in which they had grown up.

In Father's case I think it was a reaction to the grinding poverty in his parents' home and the piety with which Grandfather accepted it. Father was the first young person in the neighborhood to go away to school, and to his last day he regretted that he left Baker Academy after one year. But at the time he felt obligated as the oldest son to take over the desperate financial affairs of the family. The years had not made a better farmer of Benjamin. His rains came wrong, his pigs wouldn't fatten properly, his calves got the "scours," his harness perversely fell apart. Besides all that, he himself was often ill with grippe, pneumonia, or bronchitis. Some of this might nowadays be diagnosed as psychosomatic. Or it may be that the granddaughter who once worked for a lung specialist is right in believing that it was a "typical fibrosed tuberculosis." In any case, he was often "laid up for a long spell." And he was sometimes away holding revival meetings.

When Father took over the reins, the slack went out of them in a hurry. Organizing his younger brothers into a working team, he routed them out of bed early and drove them and himself late. At the time the brothers resented his authority, which greatly added to the general Dungan commotion. Many were the tales they later told of this period, sometimes roaring with laughter and sometimes still half-resentful. When I remember how barely I endured my own teen-agers' in-fighting, I marvel that Grandmother managed to survive at all.

In order to bring in some much-needed cash Father went to the county seat for a term of training called Normal, which entitled the successful student to a certificate to teach the rural schools of the county. He taught at least three terms, in a school close to his parents' home. He liked teaching and was good at it, a fact later attested by his success in getting his daughters through the thickets of fractions and ratios. But then as now, teaching was not a well-paid occupation and a young man bent on getting ahead left it as soon as he could.

Eventually be began to buy a half-section of land near his parents' home and to accumulate livestock and implements for working it. When he wasn't in the fields, he was intently studying materials from the state agricultural college. Long before any one else in the neighborhood, he had a pedigreed bull and boar. He was also, I think, the first to put out alfalfa. In short, he set out to wring success from the situation at hand, a hill farm in Southeast Kansas. Five generations of his Dungan ancestors had moved toward one seductive Western horizon after another, but he would fight it out where Fate had dropped him. As it turned out he would have put together both an easier and a larger success if he *had* moved a hundred and fifty miles northwest to become a wheat grower on the rich loess soil of Central Kansas. But that he couldn't know.

In a little notebook he kept in the early years he jotted down the amount of his personal property at assessing time in March. Beginning in 1892 each notation showed an increase in the number of horses, cattle and pigs. Each year the value of taxable machinery was greater and in most years more bushels of corn were on hand. Real property grew in the same painful but steady way. By the time of his marriage in 1895 he had title (and mortgage, to be sure, though not for long) to 320 acres of land with a new three-roomed house, sheds for the livestock, and at least the minimum farm implements. Barn, orchard, windmill, fencing, big house, more land would come later.

My father — my strong, fiercely-protective, hot-tempered, repressed Gibraltar of a father! I never think of him without gratitude or without sadness. He had the gaunt, big-boned frame of the Dungan men, his mother's black hair and blunted nose ("pugged," we called it in disgust when we discovered it on our own faces), and powerful, squarish hands with very little finger dexterity. Like his father before him, he had a fine mind. But where Grandfather was easy-moving, Father was forever hurried and as often as not actually trotted about his work. Where Grandfather talked freely about his aspirations and spiritual yearnings, Father's emotions were tightly bottled, smoldering in his deep-set eyes, occasionally bursting out in a quick anger, but rarely put into words.

He too loved to read and early began to buy books as he could. Unlike his father, he was never reading when he

[33]

should have been working, though often when he should have been sleeping. After the longest days, even in haying or silo-filling times, he might read until midnight. I am still haunted occasionally by the memory of finding him late one summer night after a brutally long day's work, bent over a book at the kitchen table with gnats floating about in the yellow glow of his coal oil lamp.

He was one of the people toward whom responsibility gravitates by some law of its own. He did not go looking for it, but when it was in his vicinity he saw it and accepted it. When his father moved away, he took over church leadership, becoming trustee, Sunday School superintendent, and chief contributor. For a long time he was township road overseer and was usually on the school board, as well as representing his township on the County Central Committee of the Republican Party. He was the one who planned the programs for Memorial Day and helped clean up the cemetery, got the speaker for the Fourth of July celebrations, saw to it that the church had a new roof, helped organize the first telephone company, sent "hands" to help out a sick neighbor.

All this community work was on top of a farm routine with physical demands farmers today can scarcely imagine. He was well past thirty before he owned his first riding plow. Around and around the fields he walked with the rein over one shoulder, his feet plodding over the uneven soil, his knuckles white from holding the plow in place, his shapeless hat pulled low to protect his eyes from the fierce Kansas sun, from early morning till sundown, with only a short break at noon. After supper came the chores: the heavy harnesss to be taken from the horses and hung up, hay to be pitched down from the mow, swill to be carried to the pigs, eight or ten cows to be milked. That was the regular routine. At haying or silo-filling time the hours stretched from four in the morning until ten at night.

As the operation expanded, the farm implements acquired seats and a windmill forced water to the waiting tanks. But because the chutes he installed to simplify work with his own cattle were the only ones in the neighborhood, men brought their cattle for help in branding and dehorning, and his dipping vat required his time when other men's livestock

[34]

came to be rid of vermin. His increasing herds meant renting pasturage in a distant part of the county, which in turn meant days in the saddle for moving back and forth and for an occasional inspection. True, there were hands to help with all this, but Father took pride in pacing them, so that his output of footpounds never fell off as it should have.

In a real sense he gave his life to push himself and his children up the Ladder a bit. When pneumonia struck in late 1917 he was aged beyond his years. To be sure, pneumonia was a killer in those days. But he had been endowed with a powerful physique. If he had not abused it in pursuit of his goals, it should have seen him through even pneumonia.

*　　*　　*　　*

If Father's reaction against his parents was based on his impatience with their inability to take even the first step up the Ladder, Mother's revolt was quite different. The Halls, too, were dirt-poor, but since almost everybody else in the neighborhood was in the same condition, they saw no sensible reason to agonize over it — especially when so much fun could be had in spite of it. What nettled Mamie was not the poverty, but the limitations of her environment plus a feeling that her parents had unjustly doomed her to a tight little neighborhood where she felt she did not belong. Any amateur psychologist of today would say that she was trying to find herself.

The search would last all her life. After Father's death it would take her from Belknap to campaign for and win an elective office in the County Seat. While there she would develop the best, perhaps the only, *planned* garden in town, partly to satisfy her own aesthetic sense and partly to bring admiring visitors. Eventually the search would take her to an apartment in Wichita, where before her death in 1936 she had begun to achieve local recognition as a collector of antique glass.

I think she never felt that she found out where she was supposed to be, but wherever she went hunting for it her heels carried her lightly and swiftly. Perhaps what she really wanted was distinction. Whatever it was, she had a good deal of fun chasing it and it kept her running almost until death

[35]

*"Aunt Ida" — Ida Dungan Beloof,
born in 1883, once ran for
governor of Kansas
on the Socialist ticket.*

*Julia Kimerlin Hall,
maternal grandmother*

Mamie Hall Dungan
about age 20

Twenty-five years later,
styles had changed,
but Mamie Dungan remained a
beautiful woman

C. O. Dungan,
about age 49,
just before he died

caught her. She who used to drive a horse seven tedious miles and back for a chance to listen to a musical program on the old Chautauqua circuit would have *loved* the excitements of today. Not long before her death she said of the tumult shaping up in the mid-Thirties, "I hope I can live to see how all this comes out." It was no tame spirit we drew for a mother.

When Juliet took her second husband, Mother was only a few weeks old. With the best of motives the couple proceeded to do the infant a disservice which colored her whole life. One can almost hear the new husband coaxing: "Look, Julie, you and I will probably have children. I already love little Mamie as if she were my own. Let's never let her know she isn't my child. That way she will not think of me as only a stepfather."

To this plan Grandmother, young and by temperament willing for her man to do her thinking, agreed. She even consented to burn Howard's honorable discharge papers, and when his family tried to establish contact with his child, she prevented them from doing so. In two strokes Mother always felt she was denied a chance for a wider life than was possible in the Belknap neighborhood. (How exalted she would have been if she could have known that one of her daughters would live for considerable periods in Europe and the Near East and that three of them would one day rendezvous in Rome!)

Hall never got around to a legal adoption; in fact the very possibility of such a step probably never occurred to him. (Which is why Mother had to be married under a name different from the one she had always used.) True to their resolution, neither Ezra nor Juliet ever spoke to Mother about the former marriage. He was, she always conceded, never unkind to her and in fact showed marked favoritism to her.

But somehow, in the mysterious way by which children absorb information they are not supposed to get, she very early knew in the core of her being that there was something unusual in her family relationship. Somewhere she picked up the word "bastard" and fastened upon it, without understanding that even if she were born before her parents' marriage no taint of illegitimacy was involved. She *felt* different

[38]

and she knew she *was* different from the two brothers and sister who came along in good time. The difference, she grew up thinking, was that she was that dreadful, disgraceful thing that people didn't talk about.

Because her parents were basically kind and loving people, she missed the worst damage which might have been ·done. Even so, her response to her imagined stigma affected her whole life pattern. How much of the response was physical there is, of course, no way of knowing. Like her mother she was slight and allergic, developing asthma in middle age, and finally emphysema. All her life she was an easy target for prowling microbes, quite without the kind of stamina the Dungans had by birthright.

But one does not have to speculate about the response of her spirit. In her effort to prove to the world that she was indeed different from those about her, she reached out hungrily for experience, snatching it where and as she could find it. The family lived near a camp ground on the old Osage Trail, up which passed movers' wagons and other travelers to make connections with the Santa Fe Trail. With her younger brother she hung about the camp, listening with greedy ears to the travelers' stories of other places and ways of living. She read whatever print came to hand. She learned to sew and to groom herself fastidiously and she developed a sense of style which went far beyond her mother's willingness to wear old finery if that was all that could be had. She was pretty and animated — and absolutely determined to "do something and be somebody," as she later admonished her daughters. In fact, she was one of the few people I've known whose appetite for life might fairly be called insatiable. An incident near the end of her life illustrates the point. She had gone to visit a daughter in Washington, D.C., and found her house bound with an ailing baby and complaining of boredom.

"You with your university degree bored?" she snapped. "If I couldn't do anything else, I'd get to be the best bridge player in the crowd."

The "difference" had plenty of time to fester in her, for she was past ten before her misunderstanding was discovered during a household drama then commonplace. In those days it was considered necessary to "break a child's will" so that his obedience could be counted on to be "instant and unquestioning." Susanna Wesley, that redoubtable mother of John and Charles and seventeen others, put this basic principle of child training into words for all time: "In order to form the minds of children, the first thing to be done is to conquer their will and bring them to an obedient temper. To inform the understanding is a work of time and must, with children, proceed by slow degrees as they are able to bear it: *but the subjection of the will is a thing that must be done at once and the sooner the better.*" (Italics mine.)

Three-year-old Dency had been guilty of some infantile crime, or perhaps merely of the general obstreperousness for which the age is noted. Grandmother had decided that the time for will-breaking had arrived. Like most older sisters, Mamie was devoted to the family baby. When the whip began to flail, she threw herself into its arc and around the little sister, screaming wildly, "I don't care if I am a bastard, you can't do this to Dency."

Grandmother was so astounded that the switch fell out of her hand and the culprit slid off scot free. The long overdue explanations settled one issue in Mamie's mind and opened up several new ones. At the time she was too young to do more than ply her mother with questions about her father and his family. Since Grandmother was on the defensive she undoubtedly did not minimize the quality of either, thus reinforcing the sense of "difference" in another way.

As the child grew older and realized what the destruction of the military papers and prevention of contact with her father's family "back East" had really meant, she became resentful. The pension she might have had would have helped her to an education and the shadowy family might have taken her into a wider world. Or so she felt — and was all the more determined that her daughters would not get stuck in Belknap. The result was that at least two of us always seemed to ourselves to be marooned, to be merely waiting to get "out."

Mamie's childhood was not bleakly unhappy. It was spent in a household not unduly crowded; a total of four children in that time and place was practically race suicide. Deprivations were common to all the neighborhood children and were therefore accepted as the natural order of things. Juliet was a fine cook, Kentucky style, and her family loved to eat. Knowing what pretty clothes mean to a little girl, she did the best she could for her two. And Mother enjoyed the singing and joking as much as any one.

The neighborhood itself was not without excitements. Indians, for instance. Living so close to a trail much used by the Osages, the family had frequent visits from them.

"They came mostly at meal time," Mother used to tell us, voice and hands dramatizing in the way of a born storyteller. "A big red fellow would walk right in without knocking and say, 'How.' Your grandfather would tell him 'How,' and then our caller would ask for food and your grandfather would wave to him to wait. We children would eat as fast as we could, because after all, an Indian was an Indian and if you were as full of big-bad-Injun stories as we were, you never knew what might happen. When we were through, your grandfather would give him a sign and he'd sweep every crumb of food into his blanket and stalk out."

The memory of one particular visit, when she was about nine, stayed with her always and never failed to bring the hair up on our young scalps when she described it. Her parents were away somewhere with the two younger children, leaving her and Charlie at home. Suddenly the dog set up the wild yelping which heralded the approach of a certain type of visitor, then disappeared with all possible dispatch. The children knew what this meant. They ran to bolt the door, then crawled up into the loft of the cabin. Through a crack in the mortar they watched three burly Indians ride around the farmyard calling, "Holl-oo, holl-oo." Frightened beyond moving, the children dropped their heads and lay flat on the floor. Presently the shouts were close and accompanied by great banging and yanking on the bolted door. The children felt their hearts beating so loudly that they were sure the Indians must know that they were in the house. The banging and bawling grew so furious the children were convinced that the door would give way.

"If they find we were here all the time and didn't let them in," Mamie whispered, "they may scalp us."

Trembling and barely able to speak, the two children tot-

[41]

tered down the stair and found the strength to open the door.

"How!" Mamie managed to say politely.

Then, blessed relief. In a mixture of signs and mono-syllables the callers gave the children a message for the squaws and papooses following in wagons. The children were so relieved that they handed over a pan of fresh gingerbread without protest and were not much scolded for their gen-erosity when their mother returned.

Through her adolescence and young womanhood, the con-flict between Mother and her parents intensified. They said, truthfully, that she was "not strong" and should take care of herself. She annoyed them by refusing to be coddled. They pointed out, also truthfully, that spunky, headstrong girls hardly ever come to a good end. She took the bit in her teeth and somehow got off to "normal" to be trained for teaching, that being the likeliest route to independence and Becoming Somebody.

When she was sixteen she began to go with a dark, intense young man as determined to "get ahead" as she was to be "somebody." It was a long courtship, for both had things to do before taking on the risks of marriage. He had to lay the foundations of his farm. She had to get together decent equipment for housekeeping instead of the makeshifts with which most neighborhood brides began married life. She even began to buy an adjoining eighty acres of land. She kept on teaching, riding a horse through rain or snow, build-ing her own fires, facing a pack of "big boys," and going back to Normal during summers until she had accumulated a reed organ, new furniture and, for the time and place, a good trousseau. Her wedding dress was made of off-white taffeta with a boned bodice so small that by the time they were fourteen not one of her daughters could squeeze into it. The dress also had a lace bertha, leg-of-mutton sleeves, and a long full skirt complete with bustle. In thumbing through the fashion books of the mid-Nineties, I marvel at her flair for style. That dress which we used to spread out and admire really *was* a knockout. I do not remember what Grandmother D always spoke of as the "infare dress," but it too was one which the elders were still talking about long after it had been consigned to the ragbag.

[42]

Perhaps the crowning example of her spunk and independence was her contracting to teach another term of school after she was married. By the mores of the neighborhood this unheard-of step amounted to a positive flouting of Providence. Before Thanksgiving she knew that the contract had been a mistake. Almost any other woman would have broken it. She continued to climb on her horse and go to work. In all the two families, only her mother-in-law was willing to admire this stubbornness, and even *she* conceded that it had been risky. "Sure and I was relieved when that term of school was over," she often told me," and she could take off her corset and stay off her horse."

Such were the man and woman who in August, 1895, took each other for better or worse until death should part them. It goes without saying that no slack, easy-going child would ever spring from this union.

We who appeared were not only not easy-going; we were not easy-coming. Clambering on each other's heels at unreasonably short intervals, we all got a bad mauling during the long, difficult deliveries occasioned by Father's big bones and Mother's small pelvis. The deliveries were effected at home, on her own bed, without any pain killer. Years later when a sixth child was born and the doctor used chloroform, she marveled at the bliss of drifting off into oblivion without "having to go to work on the shoulders when I finally had the head."

There were four little girls of us in the first round then, after ten years, a boy and in two more years, another girl. The second family, coming when I was already away at school for nine months of the year, had little part in shaping my life. During their early years the family frost blossoms were either my adored little darlings or my pesky little nuisances, depending on their behavior and my mood. They were outside the sibling pull and haul in which personality is shaped. Not until they were nearing adulthood did the usual brother-sister relationship develop between us.

We in the first four could thank Mother's appetite for novels plus her craving for distinction for the fact that only one of us got one of the time-honored names assembled in the back of the dictionary.

[43]

Avis — so unusual that when I first saw an auto-lending agency's advertisement that "Avis goofed," I recoiled with an automatic "Now what did I do?" And all my life I've had to face the question, "Long or short *a*?" — an issue not completely resolved to this day, because I failed to take a forthright stand when I went away to school at age thirteen.

And then there was *Hildred,* a real puzzler. Mildred, of course, but where did that *H* come from? In fifty years of moving about the country, I have known just one other Hildred besides my sister. It sounds Scandinavian, but I've never known or read of a Swede, Dane, or Norwegian burdened with it. It was so hard for children to say that for many years we called her "Hoodie," and later the oil men among whom she worked settled for "Hilda."

The fourth little girl fared worst of all. *Idylene* — a real soul-crusher of a name. True, I must take some of the blame for it, because during the fall before her birth I went with my parents to a Sunday School Convention in Topeka. While they struggled with whatever delegates to Sunday School Conventions then struggled with, I played with a little girl named "Idylene." Later when I heard discussions of a name for the new baby, Mother always claimed that I suggested my playmate's name. But I have always maintained that she could and would have quashed the idea if she hadn't liked it.

The little girl who got the sensible name, Irene, alas, did not live to grace it. Diphtheria took her in the spring of 1907 when she was eight. There was then no such thing in the world as immunization against the dread disease, but an anti-toxin was available as a treatment. It was, however, new and the country doctor was afraid of it. In spite of adult efforts to keep the rest of us well away from the sickroom, there came a day when through a half-open door I had a glimpse of Mother kneeling beside a bed with her face buried in golden curls and an arm flung out over an unearthly quiet figure. I shall never forget that moment — or how far away from us our neighbors stood at the cemetery. An evil time.

In a day or two Hildred and Idylene were stricken. Father insisted that the doctor use the anti-toxin, and they were speedily well again, giving the parents the bitter knowledge that the first death had probably been unnecessary. Through it all I moved unscathed. I resented the sassafras tea they forced upon me in the hope of building up my "resistance."

As if my driving young parents, always with twice the program laid out that they could comfortably carry, did not have enough of such troubles as panics and droughts, they had *us*. I, to be sure, was hardy enough in the early years, sporting only a normal quota of runny noses and stubbed toes. The only illness I can remember before I was seven was an occasional croup — remembered only because Grandmother's and Father's standard remedy was a towel wrung out of ice-water (a supply of which was always handy in the kitchen water-bucket) and clapped inexorably around a warm little throat. With that towel in prospect there was no temptation whatever to fake a croupy cough.

Kansas family medicine in the early twentieth century was a time of drastic remedies. For a cold there was a fiery mustard plaster or quinine taken without benefit of capsule. For rheumatism there was a liniment guaranteed to assault all nostrils for hours. And if a child looked what Grandmother H called "puny" and Grandmother D called "peek-ed" there was a big dose of castor oil, gulped in coffee or fruit juice and precariously kept down by a shuddering stomach.

The appearance of any unfamiliar set of symptoms meant a careful consultation of a thick book known to us as "the Doctor Book." If this research made the symptoms seem ominous there was, before the arrival of the telephone, a hurried trip to Moline to "fetch" our portly old doctor, who counted a pulse while watching an impressively fat gold watch, studied the patient's tongue, laid an ear over a heart and in some cases palpated a chest. Then, examination completed, he counted out some pills or poured some liquid, chucked any small bystanders under the chin and went out to his buggy. About the same proportion of his patients got well as do today after three or four days in a hospital "for tests."

When I was seven my sturdiness came to a sudden end. About the first of December I came down with pneumonia. In those days the disease was a nightmare to those who stood around a bedside. There was so little they could do but pray and sponge the burning skin. But if all went well the

[45]

"crisis" came in a few days and after a while the patient was good as new.

It didn't work out well in my case. I developed a "lung abscess," perhaps what is now known as empyema, and lay for weeks between life and death. Two other doctors were brought in one day to decide whether or not to open the chest. I remember hearing them "consult" beside my bed on the supposition that I was too young or too sick to understand. They decided that I couldn't stand the operation. After all, the choice would be between doing it there on the kitchen table or trying to transport me fifty miles to the nearest hospital.

I continued to lie abed, with anxious parents, grandparents, uncles, and aunts hovering over me and young sisters pushed into the background. Eventually the abscess must have become walled off, because I was able to be up. By then Mother was dangerously ill with a miscarriage and a high fever, so that the house quivered with anxiety.

One warm April day a fit of hard coughing ruptured the abscess. The pus came up in mouthfuls and I had to sleep sitting up lest I drown in it, as Father was later to do. Eventually I exhausted the abscess and began to get well. But my chubby person was thereafter thin and tense, I caught every cold in the vicinity and rarely quelled it short of bronchitis. What may have been some food allergies appeared, leading the doctor to remark that some children just seemed to have delicate stomachs. From having been immune to the childhood diseases I was wide open.

But most important of all was learning the uses of ill health. I, who had felt outside the family, became its unquestioned center, and for several winters I couldn't help knowing that I was closely watched. In the years of young adulthood I missed a thorough neurasthenia by a narrow margin — maybe didn't miss it at all!

Hildred was no doubt conceived too soon after Mother's battle with typhoid. She screamed with colic for months and topped off her infancy with a nearly fatal burn. Both she and Irene were given to tonsillitis, toothache, and the earaches which in those days usually went on to a ruptured drum. And since there was no such thing in all the world as aspirin, let alone antibiotics, the sleepless parents sometimes in desperation gave the only pain-killer there was — laudanum. But being up-to-date, they had no truck with paregoric and never thrust a pacifier, much less a "sugar tit" into a screeching baby's mouth, as most of their neighbors did when the situation got bad.

Idylene had her share of sore throats, but distinguished herself chiefly by being exceedingly high-strung and excitable — "nervous," her sisters said. Years later Grandmother D used to chuckle about the time when the child complained of "feeling nervous" and went out to her pony. "In less than you could wink," she explained, "sure she came pounding down the road past the house, a switch flying and that pony running hell for leather, its heels going rattle-dy-bang on the bridge over the creek."

The same Indian pony developed a rascally habit of pitching the child off every time they got on plowed ground, though luckily no place else. The pony's performance never failed to set off a fine spasm of temper. No wonder the parents decided to teach her at home until she was nearly eight, rather than subject her to the rigors of an ungraded school.

While all this was going on the farm was getting bigger and the livestock more numerous. That meant hired hands and kitchen help. However, as soon as the little girls could function, the kitchen help departed.

Mamie Dungan was not one to compromise. Her neighbors might use oil cloth, but the least she would settle for was white cotton damask. Not even red or blue checks would do. Other "front rooms" might be carpeted in rag rugs woven by a neighboring woman, but ours had a store-bought Ingram carpet, a soft green with pinkish flowers. Very elegant, we children thought.

Nothing was ever wasted in those households. When a calico dress or shirt was completely worn out, it was torn into inch-wide strips, the ends of which were sewn together, and then the whole long string wound into a ball, to become the woof on the rug loom. Tiny scraps of new materials were carefully saved against the day when they would be "pieced" into a quilt. Quite small girls could work on the "rag balls," but their mothers usually considered them un-

[47]

trustworthy at quilt making. Their hand-sewn seams refused to stay put!

Other little girls might wear pigtails and have them combed maybe twice a week, but our hair was often put up on curlers and was brushed to fine luster every day. Some little girls might wear rags and tags, but not Mamie Dungan's, even in a day when nothing but shoes and stockings were bought in stores.

To start from the skin, we wore panties and panty-waists, all homemade from muslin or nainsook. Each "waist" for each of four girls had four handmade buttonholes and seven handsewn buttons. The panties each had six buttonholes and were decorated with tucks and lace or embroidery. Next came a four-button slip which the grandmothers called a "shimmy," also of muslin or nainsook, with a decorative edging at the neck, arm holes and hem. On summer Sundays we added a lace-trimmed petticoat under our frilly best dresses, so that we would be sure not to "show through."

Our everyday wear was a long way from the easy-do of blue jeans and tee-shirt. Above the handmade underwear was a "sack apron" with heaven knows how many buttons down the back, a homemade jacket or coat when needed, topped off with a homemade sunbonnet in the summer or hood in the winter. Our trusty old White sewing machine was rarely closed. If ever a treadle needed its touted ball bearings, that one did. I never recall it without blessing the invention of nylon tricot.

The relationships within the family were unusual. Neither my sisters nor I can remember a blow-up between our parents. We can't even remember a minor clash, let alone heated disagreement between them about the management of the family.

What does this mean? A couple as driving and quick-tempered as these two must have had disagreements. As one long and well-married, I *know* there must have been times when feelings were hurt and harsh things were said. Yet none of us can dredge up a memory of such times. Does this mean that they were better at dissembling than most couples? I think not, for if there was one thing Father couldn't do, it was dissemble. He was a Dungan, as incapable of a tiny white lie as a black whopper.

Or does it mean that they thought it important to put up a harmonious front before their young? Or that we, more than most children, wished not to perceive tension? What I do know is that the apparent totality of their accord was troubling as well as comforting. Their very unanimity multiplied parental power and made either rebellion or playing off one against the other unthinkable. Discipline was no problem in our family. One silent, contemptuous look from Father was enough to chill the marrow of any young miscreant — and Mother never lessened the effect by so much as a fleeting smile. She left us absolutely out in the temporary cold.

The result was predictable. "Talking back" was an unknown delight. Not for us the good shout back over shoulders while we shot through a door released with a heart-warming bang. My children did it to me some times, but it wasn't done to their maternal grandparents. (Or paternal, either, for that matter!) "Honor thy father and thy mother" was Law, part of the Ten Commandments themselves, age-old and immutable. We would have as soon disputed the rising of tomorrow's sun as Father's oracular, "Mother knows best," or the reverse by Mother. I still remember the profound shock with which I first heard an adolescent friend declare that she not only didn't like her parents but thought them downright stupid. Parents had stature in those days.

As for a special class of humanity known as "teen-agers," neither the word nor the concept existed. A youth remained under parental control as long as the parents could control him. Common gossip in the neighborhood was of parents who used the buggy whip on their rebellious young males, until the boys grew so big that they either left home or bested their father at fisticuffs. There was almost no corporal punishment in our home. With Father's "look" available there didn't need to be.

Did they really see eye to eye on all the decisions they had to make? They couldn't have, and yet they seemed to and without either seeming to dominate the other. One device which they used was a consistent sharp division of areas of jurisdiction. Mother was absolute sovereign in the house and in all matters of dress and behavior. Father was in complete

[49]

charge from the front door to the farthest fence. When a no-man's land occasionally appeared he said, "Go ask your mother," or she said, "You'll have to talk to Papa about that." It took us a long time to realize that talking to the second parent would get us no immediate answer — that we were being put off until they could find privacy to make a joint decision.

Perhaps the singleness of their purpose to get ahead and to push their daughters ahead was a factor in their unanimity. Their basic goals and to some extent their values were the same. Although she had come up in a family given to fun and frolic, she seemed to have wholly renounced Hall ways. I never heard her protest the rigidity of Dungan mores. Not until long after father's death did we discover that she knew the taste of Benedictine or could do a good schottische. If he seemed remote and austere to us, he was anything but that to her. Occasionally she embarrassed my little Puritan self by dropping flirtatiously upon his knee and tweaking his nose or ear. I have the impression that she also embarrassed him — such goings-on before the children!

Another unusual feature in the family relationships lay in the handling of money. I never heard either parent protest the other's spending habits. If she complained when he bought a complete Shakespeare or he when she took to a style promulgated by the *Delineator Magazine,* it was not within earshot of little pitchers. Perhaps the very absence of cash accounted for its not being a source of family friction. Twice a year, when a shipment of porkers went to Kansas City and once a year when young beefs followed suit, money was deposited in the bank, but nobody saw anything, not even a piece of paper. The weekly can of cream brought in just enough to pay for flour, sugar, coffee and a few other staples. The rest of our food was produced on the farm. Dry goods and hardware were "charged" until the next dispatch of livestock. Then Father went around and settled all the accounts, and we began charging again. He paid his hired men by check, and if the bank account ran out, the banker "carried" him.

Nothing much was ever said to us about the handling of money — we simply knew that nobody in his right mind spent such a scarce commodity carelessly. Hildred squeezed a dime harder than the rest of us but got no special parental citations for her thrift. Actually, we had little need for money. We couldn't spend it till we got to town, and in town we could always charge what we really needed — and the gulf between desire and need was both clearly and early understood.

But, of course, there were no cokes, no merry-go-round, no movies, no short-lived plastic toys, no ice-cream wagons. Candy was a weekly treat, bought a few sticks at a time — peppermint striped, lemon, horehound, or licorice. In fact, commercialized enticement for the youthful purse was an art yet unborn. Children in our neighborhood had plenty of troubles but among them the lack of pocket money ranked very low indeed.

At about age thirteen (probably then because that was the year when I, the oldest, went away to school so equipped) each of us in turn was given access to the checkbook. No individual accounts were ever set up for us. We simply began to write checks on the family account. So far as I know, none of us ever abused this unorthodox system of family finance. In fact, we did not realize that there was anything unusual about it until we were away from home and could begin to compare notes with contemporaries.

*   *   *

In this age of psychologizing no family can be described without some attention to the unconscious stresses within it, especially those which later show up as hostility.

Not until I was past thirty and had devoured enough **Freud & Co.** to be able to ask myself *why* I had made a wounding remark to a sister whom I loved did I realize how jealous my child-self was of the little girl who was Hildred. Just to ask the question made me realize that this was not the first occasion on which I had surprised myself with a comment outwardly innocent but aimed, I had *almost* been aware, at a spot where she was especially vulnerable. This sudden perception drove me, literally *drove* me to answer: "You seem to want to hurt or embarrass her." That only drove in another question: "But *why* do I want to hurt her?"

[51]

Out of all the books I could answer obliquely and without real personal engagement: "Usually when people act that way they actually do want to hurt some one." The words came easily enough, out of the books, but their impact was stunning. My image of myself as a morally rather superior young woman was stripped away. I saw myself in a new light, and the seeing had the crushing force Grandfather used to say accompanied his "coming under the conviction of sin." For several days thereafter I went about my usual routine, busily remembering and putting the puzzle together.

Today's parents may be exasperated with the manifestations of "sibling rivalry," but they have been schooled to expect it as a normal part of family living and to try to deal with it as such. In the early years of the century parents not only didn't have the comfort of the scientific-sounding phrase, they had the word of all right-minded thinkers on the subject that childish jealousies were evils to be eradicated, root and branch, as speedily as possible. The usual result was that a child preserved a tolerable image of himself by concealing from himself as much of his jealousy and hostility as possible, thereby becoming a "good," even an "unselfish" child, approved by himself and the adults who had him in charge. Sometimes he outgrew the buried rivalries. Sometimes he didn't. I had not.

The general outlines of the unconscious rancor I had carried so long were easy enough to trace as I went about my housework during the next few days. Hildred had not only displaced me as the second child always does, but her troubled infancy had kept me away from home for considerable periods. To this I could add an early-teen memory of Grandmother D telling me that when Hildred was about two, some of the young uncles thought it a joke to teach her to say, "Sister may be smart, but I'm pretty." (Was that why I had grown up feeling that anything I would ever get from life would be by being "smart?" I didn't know, but by that time I knew it was a dangerous notion for a young female to have.)

My sister certainly was pretty. She had long dark curls, where my straightish flaxen hair early turned to nondescript brown. Her skin was a delicate pink and white, while the chief virtue of my sturdy coating was that it never sunburned, no great asset in a time when all proper females warded off tanning by any device from sunbonnets to buttermilk facials. She had a dimple under each dark eye. In her "baby picture," and all the later childhood pictures, she was a little beauty.

But in the hours of horrified objectivity about myself I came to see something much more important: there was never a time when I didn't think of her as Father's favorite. Looking back as an adult, and a parent, I knew he had not played favorites, but I could also understand how a child with other imagined grievances had acquired the feeling.

Hildred, I suddenly realized, had been an unusual child, serious beyond her years — and no wonder, after her pain-filled infancy. She was practically born adult and responsible. There were no real slackers on that farm, but Idylene and I met adult demands with as much goofing-off as we felt entitled to. Hildred fell in with the parents. Very early she identified herself with them and strove to "get the work all done up and *then* rest." Our view of the matter was that morning or afternoon, summer or winter the work was *never* all done up. Why couldn't she see that, we demanded in many a fierce argument safely out of parental hearing. "Papa and Mama need us," she exhorted, while throwing her own full weight into the need. There was a limit to the time we would give before scooting out to a book or a pony. I cannot remember that either parent upbraided us, but under the circumstances Father would have been sub-human if he had not appreciated his second daughter's loyal partnership.

There was more, I realized as I tunneled back into the past. When we were a little older I often dreadfully embarrassed her. By the time I was ten and she eight, I was well entrenched in a world where I allowed no trespassers. I felt "outside" the neighborhood, perhaps partly because of Mother's determination that we would escape Belknap. But to some extent I also felt different from and outside the family. I had already learned the value of quick, pert chatter as a device for keeping people out of my holy of holies. There was as yet no such word as "wise-crack," but if there had been, any discerning adult would have noted that I was trying my silly best to develop the skill. I had learned to enjoy playing with words, and more important, that I could

[53]

sometimes bring adults to a roar of laughter. When they were laughing at my sallies, there was no chance of their poking into areas where I considered they had no business being. By age ten I had created for myself a mask. I knew, or almost knew, that I had done it. To outsiders this made me something of a show-off. To myself it was protective coloration, though of course I didn't use those weighty words.

Brother Horace Dungan
at age 15.

Sister Marjorie Dungan
about age 14.

But nobody, certainly no child, can hit the bull's eye every time. I made a full quota of what are now known as "bloopers," but were then called "breaks." If you made a really bad break you never heard the last of it.

On such occasions Hildred considered that I was not only a chatterbox and Smart Aleck, but pretty close to a liar because I exaggerated and made things up. I was a blemish on the family honor. In order to curb the "feistiness" which caused her so much embarrassment she often berated me soundly and lengthily. And if vainglory brought me to an abasing fall, she was quick to point out the lesson and slow to let me forget it. When the inevitable happened after I had tottered up on new ice skates to announce that I was about to "cut a figure eight" she led the younger girls in a chorus of hoots. Thereafter, any boastful statement of intention was treated to an ego-shrinking, "Yes, you'll cut a figure eight."

It took me a while to explore the dark chambers of this ancient estrangement. But the search and the turn-about toward freedom were the first steps toward health at a time when I badly needed to take them.

Many more years had to pass before amused observation of a grandson's zealous efforts to "catch up with" his older sister taught me to understand the forces which must have been at work in little girls who shared parents but, as always among siblings, only partly shared experience.

postscripta, 1975

As it turned out, of course, the Dungans arguing so passionately in 1912 might have saved their breath. Debs got nowhere except prison, Teddy Roosevelt and Taft killed each other off, and Woodrow Wilson came in trailing the income tax and national prohibition, though the latter was not his doing. During his first term we got our first Model T and an Edison phonograph which all too soon was playing, "Pack Up Your Old Kit Bag." By 1912 the handwriting of Today was appearing, if only we had had the wit to see it.

* * * *

My penchant for "playing with words" may have landed me in childish troubles, but it also got me my first article in

Harper's Magazine before I was thirty, and soon into enough other magazines to allow me to call myself a "free lancer." The money came in very handy during the Depression.

* * * *

Cynthia's refusal to vote after a lifetime of campaigning was put to good use forty years later, when I was president of the St. Louis League of Women Voters. One of my activities was talking to small groups on the good League subject, "Is Politics Your Job?" I warmed up many an audience with the story of Grandmother's refusal to avail herself of the privilege she had so long sought. It never failed to get a laugh and I never failed to point the moral: "She wasn't so different from many of us today — she wanted the privilege but not the responsibility."

* * * *

Over the years the Dungan teetotalism has dimmed. For Idylene in the cocktail parties of Washington, Athens, Brussels, and Rome, where her husband was stationed at various times; for me in the less glamorous parties of St. Louis, where my husband's work as a regional attorney for the National Labor Relations Board insured that usually there would be present one or more union business agents or Vice-Presidents in Charge of Personnel, or often both! For the youngest members of the family a before-dinner relaxer became more or less routine. Hildred stuck closer to the faith. But then she never had a husband's interests to promote. One year of high school teaching was enough to let her know that teaching was not for her. After a secretarial course her first job was with one of the most colorful individuals in a colorful breed of entrepreneur then living in Texas, Oklahoma and Kansas — an "independent oil man." This one had managed to scrape together equipment and leases to drill his first wildcat. It "came in big," and he went on to others still bigger. As his business grew, Hildred became office manager and then secretary-treasurer of the corporation he founded — and learned to talk of "the Majors" with much the same feeling as Grandfather exhibited when speaking of the Prince of Evil. Of all my grandfather's direct descendants, who must now number well over a hundred, there are, I think, no alcoholics. When I consider the national average for that disease, I tip a hat to Benjamin and Cynthia and the noisy, opinionated crew they produced.

3

The Farm

In the making of a life, setting is only slightly less important than the cast of characters. For a farm child in the century's first decade, setting was much more important than it is now. Today's country child goes to school and church in the nearest town. Because little if any of his food is produced on the farm, his chores are few. Because tilling and harvesting are done by big, expensive machines, the farm must be large, but hired help does not become part of the family. Most important of all, his isolation is gone, swallowed up by gasoline engine, radio and television. His life differs little from that of his town or suburban cousin.

It was very different with us. We *lived* on that stretch of hill and bottom land with a wooded creek running through it. I can remember when the men of the neighborhood dug the holes and tamped in the poles for the first telephone line and how exciting it was when the first calls began to come in, and how we raced to be the one to listen in on a neighbor's conversation. I can even remember when the wonderful Rural Free Delivery, or "mail route" as it was known, first made its appearance on the dusty road at the end of our lane and gave Father the means to subscribe to the Topeka Daily Capitol instead of the weekly to be picked up at the postoffice when we went to town.

At least until we could read proficiently, we lived and had our whole being on those acres.

A road bisected the property, or what we called a road, running close in front of the house to join the main road to town just at the creek crossing. In the beginning, when the babies were coming and the economic struggle was severest, the house had consisted of three good-sized rooms strung along end to end. By the time I can remember a lean-to had been added to house the hired men. Later a two-storied frame house with a wide back porch was built.

Back of the house rose a steep hill with outcroppings of big, weathered rocks and a "hog fence" running over its crest. Eventually, almost every field and pasture was made either hog-tight or hog-proof. Our living might come partly from hogs, but we wanted them strictly in their place. To us the hill seemed enormous, something just short of the mountains whose pictures we saw in storybooks. Climbing up to pick the first spring flowers or to take the view was a favorite pastime.

Angling back into the hill was a dog-legged cave scooped out by Father and his men after a cyclone which devastated two or three neighboring farms. Most farmers had "caves" in those days, innocent places dug a few feet into the earth and reached by a few descending steps. Our cave was different. It was bored into the hill, turned a corner, bored again, and turned another corner, all the time getting darker. It was a fearsome place, silent and damp, with the heavy smell of earth mold to remind a child of something she couldn't identify. A blacksnake was reputed to reside above the planks which formed the low ceiling. Though nobody ever saw the snake, we all firmly believed in his existence. But I don't think the possible presence of a creature everybody assured us was absolutely harmless was what made that hole in the ground so fearful a place. I only know that if some one had clapped the door shut to confine me in that black hole I would have been reduced to shrieking panic. A pair of neighbor boys, visiting with their mother, provided me with an early introduction to the peculiarity of male psychology when they shouted joyfully at the discovery of a perfect place for hiding during "Run sheep run." They even pulled the door shut behind themselves!

The narrow back yard was paved in flat stones pried out of the hill. We never heard the word "patio," but we had one thirty years before the rest of America. There we played on muddy days and there was swung an enormous black kettle for heating washday water every week and making the year's supply of laundry soap. On the retaining wall which held back the hill we could balance and skitter until some adult caught us. The rocks were "laid up," not cemented.

The front doorstep was a huge slab of red sandstone, taken from the hill and undoubtedly shaped and evened by a neighbor who laid up stone fences around his own holdings. No Dungan ever had the skill or patience to achieve such a doorstep.

Honeysuckle bushes sprawled over the front yard fence, and a line of roses fanned down toward the vegetable garden. In one corner, near a huge lilac bush, was a well, with a windlass and bucket that all too soon began to represent Duty. Just outside the side gate was the woodpile, bane of every farm child's existence in those days. Any stove which must provide for farm workers and a flock of growing children had a greedy maw. Black walnut and oak were considered to make the cleanest, hottest fires, but they also made the heaviest carrying and somehow the woodbox seemed able to swallow more of them than of more light-weight woods.

Across the road and down a way was the barn, with bins for grain, pegs for saddles and harness, stalls for a dozen or so horses, and a mow full of hay, scratchy and smelly but wonderful to tumble in. Beside the barn was a long shed to shelter the milk cows in winter. Back of it was the corral with a chute for use at branding and dehorning time. A big wooden silo, held together like a monster keg with metal hoops, eventually came into being and with it an annual orgy of excitement when perhaps eighteen men gathered to fill it and then came to the kitchen to fill themselves.

Right in the middle of the barnyard was the feed mill which Father installed during the early years and which involved the most irksome task to darken my childhood. He would pour a quantity of grain into the hopper, hitch a patient old horse to the end of the mill arm, and lift me or whichever child was at hand into a box he had fastened to the arm. I (or she) was then provided with a stick to keep the horse circling.

On the times when I was nabbed for the dreary rounds it seemed that my fate was far worse than the horse's. He only had to work, but I had to sit still. Just as time seemed never to admit a stop, Father would pour in more corn. The fact that he had planted it, kept it free from weeds while it grew, shucked it, run it through a hand-driven corn sheller, and was now carrying it a hundred or so pounds at a time, meant nothing to a child stiff with sitting and boredom. After not too many years the mill was abandoned as too slow for the amount of feed required.

Directly across from the house was the orchard. Father's hungry pioneer childhood had fixed in him the conviction that it was impossible to have too many food sources at hand. So, like Johnny Appleseed, he planted fruit trees — and, unlike Johnny, somehow found time to tend them. Thus we had apples from the first Maiden Blush in June to the last Winesap in the autumn and apples from the pit all winter; red and purple plums, quantities of apricots, early and late cherries, and peaches from June to late September.

The peaches were especially important in our lives for two reasons. One was that people came from miles around to buy them and they always brought along their children to help with the picking. The other was considerably less pleasant. Apples could be kept in a pit, but peaches had to be either dried or canned. Much work either way.

The fruit trees were wonderful to smell in the spring, pleasent to climb at any time, but oh, the work they made for woman and child! Fresh cherry pies are delectable, but when the cherries must first be picked, one by insignificant one, then pitted, one by squirting one, and finally enclosed in a home-made crust and baked in a hand-fired oven, they represent an amount of time and energy my daughter never has to consider.

East of the house, down the long slope to the creek, were the beehives from which Father coolly took gallons of honey each year, but where I never went, having inherited a grandmother's sensitivity to insect venom. Below the hives were the vegetable garden and the berry patches. How the little girls hated those berry patches! No berry is easily picked; some are meaner than others. They all involved stooping, chigger bites and a mulch in which snakes were said to lurk. If a berry was on the market Father coveted it and soon had it. So we had them all — strawberries, gooseberries, blackberries, dewberries, and raspberries. And the picking, compensated at the rate of ten cents a gallon was only the beginning of the work which had to be lavished on them before they met their end crushed in a bowl with sugar and thick cream or cushioned in pie crust or canned for winter sauce or jellied for hot biscuits.

The vegetable garden was Father's domain and therefore generous in proportion and yield. Cabbage and tomato plants went in by what seemed hundreds to a little girl following along to pour a dipper of water into the hole he gouged out for the plant. A succession of bean and pea plantings; two sowings of turnips; radishes and lettuce; two or three long rows of cabbages; potatoes to last the year; black-eyed peas; even popcorn went into that garden. Sweet corn, pumpkins and squash were wedged into the regular corn fields.

Children were not expected to do much tending of the garden, partly because Father spaced his rows so that a horse-drawn cultivator could be used as much as possible and partly because a hoe in the hands of a child is apt to be quick death to beans as well as weeds. But quite young children can pick beans and peas, pull radishes, and "scratch out" new potatoes. And on our farm quite young children did! In fact, a chore, lowering over all summer mornings, right after breakfast dishes and cleaning the lamp chimneys, was getting in the day's vegetables. After the beans were in the kitchen they had to be washed and snapped; peas had to be

[61]

shelled, potatoes peeled. Women who touch a button on an electric can opener or slit off the top of a frozen dab of food have no idea of what cooking was like in those days — nor, for that matter, how much better the flavor of the end product.

Below the garden ran a creek which threaded back through the farm in a long uncertain course marked by woodlots inhabited by scolding squirrels and by wading pools where minnows and sunfish tantalized us. There was also a place or two where we could take off our dresses and splash about in our underwear, pretending that we were swimming. None of us acquired that skill until we were away from home, partly because the only water deep enough was the pond, taboo because a young hand from Missouri had drowned in it, and partly because nobody ever heard of a swimming class.

The pond was one of our special places, and not only because of the fatal accident. Occasionally wild ducks settled on it for a few days. It was the only spot on the farm which made decent ice skating during the rare cold spells. Beside it grew the best wild strawberry patch on the farm. Why should finding and picking those tart, gnarled little berries be such joy when the tame berries were next thing to a curse? Because it was a personal choice to pick them rather than a chore.

There were several woodlots with black walnut trees, redbuds, a few ash and sycamores, and elms galore. All the lots were as familiar to us as the front door yard. Wild grape vines hung in good number to provide swings and fruit, which, like the strawberries by the pond, were infinitely more delicious than the cultivated Concords.

The walnut trees were our best friends, for each fall we gathered up bushels of nuts and carted them home to dry off their vile-staining shells. Later, in preparation for a winter evening around the wood-burner, some child had to crack a pan full of nuts — and woe to her if the hammer failed to get the worrisome thick shells opened at the right places.

One autumn Father had a sawmill set up in one of the lots, and all the largest walnut and oak trees were made into studdings and "finish." What fun we had listening to the saw scream when it hit a burl. And how the carpenters who later built the big square house cursed that homegrown wood! But the house will stand until it is dynamited down.

Back up from the house, a quarter of a mile, was a small tenant house, occupied when Father was lucky enough to have a couple. Beyond it stretched the pastures. Between the two houses were corn fields. Sometimes in late August, when the corn soared high above my head, I used to walk between the rows and imagine myself in the deep forest where Hansel and Gretel were lost. How dark and green the corn forest rose above me! What if I never found my way out of it and finally lay down perishing of thirst and hunger? There may even have been some actual danger. Once when I spoke of it to Mother, she said quickly, "You know, don't you, that all you have to do is keep on going down one row and before long you will come out at the end of the field. You do know that, don't you?" I did, but it was fun pretending otherwise.

Another element in the setting was the living creatures who shared it with us. Most children have pets, and we had our share of them, even to an Indian pony so spoiled that she would walk into the house if not prevented. But it was a stock farm and crowded with animals. They were born and they had to be tended. And since some parts of the tending could be done by children, the creatures' existence was part of ours. Much of the tending was repetitive and boring, but some of it, particularly the care of the young animals, was entertaining. There are few more beguiling sights than a colt capering in a meadow or a pair of month-old calves butting each other.

Some of the tending processes involved, what to childish eyes, seemed cruelty. Like most of his fellow farmers, Father did his own veterinary surgery. A great squealing in the pig pens meant that rings were going into noses, eartips being cropped and gashes being made in scrotums. Uproar in the corral meant that more gashes were being made or horns coming off or branding irons burning into flesh. As one who paled at the prospect of a splinter removal, I hated this part of animal culture and felt some animosity toward my father for engaging in it. Later I came to realize that he hated it too and shifted as soon as he could to Black Angus cattle which have no horns.

I cite these events because it has always seemed to me that the life of yesterday's country children has been outrageously sentimentalized. One of my abiding memories is of a neighbor, whom Father did not much respect, shipping a carload of wild mustangs in from the West and bringing them to our corral to be gelded into plowhorses. It was such crude surgery that one of the horses bled to death almost in front of our house. The memory of the poor beast staggering along with blood gushing from it has haunted me over the years.

The thud of a club being used to discipline a frantic horse is another memory I wish I didn't have. And the sight and sound of a gunny bag of starving kittens we found in the hedge row because some superstitious brute thought it bad luck to kill a cat. And the look on Father's face as he sadly dropped the pitifully mewing little things into a pail of water.

It was characteristic of the person I was becoming that through all these experiences, I made no protest, no shuddering revelatory comment. I seemed to be a bystander concealing my emotion under a child's helpless detachment. But I was identifying with the suffering creature. The small bystander was developing a life-long tenderness for all creatures who must suffer and die.

Children growing up on such a farm learned about sex in unorthodox ways. They learned "where babies come from" by watching a bull mount a cow and later watching that cow expand until she seemed likely to burst. Usually they did not actually see the calf born, because cows are secretive about such matters, but they might see her expel the afterbirth, and sooner or later they were sure to see her thin again and the calf wet and unfinished looking. Such children learn that young male animals must be castrated, except for roosters which are eaten. We learned also that female animals which promised to be good brood matrons had to pay their way at the plow or in the milk lot as well as fulfilling their basic mission. Otherwise they went to market along with the surplus males or were eaten.

Before anything can be eaten it must die. This we knew very early. Meat was never for us just a pink object appearing in a butcher's shop. It might be a pig we had helped to nurse through a runt's infancy or a yearling we had driven to and from pastures since the day he first staggered to his feet and found his mother's udder.

Knowledge about sex came in other ways. Besides the ubiquitous roosters there was always a bull, a boar, and either a stallion or a jack. All of them, we were warned in grave tones, could be bad actors: "Never get off your horse when the bull is around." "Never stay on a mare if the stallion gets loose and comes at her." "Never tease the boar." "Never, never go near the jack." What does a girl-child make of such admonitions, particularly if she is a girl-child with no brothers — and particularly if all the women she knew, except her mother, referred to such creatures delicately as "the animal." She arrived at the conclusion that males are indeed *different*. She felt a little resentment that the creatures which are pampered with the best food, the least work and most comfortable stalls never have much trouble in performing their share of the reproductive process. Such favoritism never seemed quite "fair."

In all of this learning there was no instruction from adults. We learned through using our eyes and listening to stray bits of conversation not meant for our ears. And, we observed without any great amount of curiosity. The odd behavior of animals was simply the way of animals. The glimpses we caught of human sexuality was simply the odd behavior of adults — and who could account for *that?* So we were only reasonably curious. But then we hadn't been soaked from babyhood in commercialized sex. What we saw we saw and if we didn't wholly understand it, there were lots of other interesting things to observe. If sex was never discussed, it was also never snickered about.

*   *   *

We lived in and about nature. Indeed, in a very real sense, we lived *under* her. If black clouds came up in July and spewed out hail stones, the orchard was stripped bare and the corn on which the animals were to be fed was reduced

[65]

to broken, ragged canes. If on other summer days white cumulus clouds piled up mountain-high but the sky around them remained a hard blue, the pastures browned and the fields and garden became sorrowfully dying. As children we saw, of course, the parched crops and vaguely knew about the unpaid notes at the bank. But what really affected us was our parents' tautness, increasing with each rainless day. If the drought went on too long, the livestock had to be sent, long before it should have been, and thin from malnutrition, into a market depressed by the offerings of other stricken stockmen. Our parents did what they could to insulate us from such distress, but we knew. We knew.

The science of meteorology wasn't conceived. We had never heard of a cold front, much less an "adiabatic lapse rate." A man looked up at the sky and made his own guess. If he saw a blue-black cloud coming up from the Northwest, he might think, "blizzard coming" but he couldn't know until almost the hour of its striking. Then the animals must be rounded up and made snug. On such occasions no children were put on cow ponies. But we did have to round up any brainless hens and young cockerels which during the summer had taken to the trees for coolness. Climb a tree to save the life of a creature which squawks and flutters further and further out on a shaky limb, and ever after you will eat chicken with a special relish.

The seasons came and went, each with its joys and sadnesses. Spring meant flowering fruit trees and the first johnny-jump-ups and the delicious airiness of the day when we were allowed to "take off our long underwear." But it also meant branding and dehorning time, when cattle bawled from the corral in what sounded to me like agony, though adults assured me that animals did not feel pain as humans do. It was a time when calves and piglets were born, but occasionally a cow could not deliver or a sow would devour her babies. In the wink of an eye lightning could char a mulberry tree not thirty feet from where we watched. Cholera on the next farm could threaten all the porkers in our lots. A cloudburst could send our creek out over its banks, ruining our wading pools and drowning any shoats that did not get out of their wallow in time.

But the Nature we lived in had other moods. In sensing them Mother was a great help. She taught us to *listen* to the cardinal pair nesting in the walnut tree and to the meadowlark perched on a pasture fence. Because she loved them herself, she saw to it that we knew the texture of a rose petal and the velvety softness of a chick's back or the fur under a kitten's neck, that we *saw* the slow reddening of the evening sky arching at last from the western to the eastern horizon.

Patiently she honed our sense until they could give us a lifetime of pleasure. The Dungans were always too busy doing and reading for that kind of attention. Thanks to her, when I first came upon Wordsworth in a "survey course," my response to such lines as "When the earliest stars began to move among the hills" and "My heart leaps up when I behold" was almost painful in its intensity. But then without the bookish, unsensuous Dungans I would never have got to the survey course!

One of the favorite themes of reminiscing elders is the wonderful, long, winter evenings when the family gathered around a fire to entertain itself. In those days entertainment was strictly a do it yourself project. You either did it or you went without it. Such evenings did exist, when, for a few hours, Hildred's dream of "the work all done up" materialized. Father would put a big chunk of black oak or black walnut into the stove and presently the heat would be right for popcorn in a wire basket at the end of a long stick. A bowl of apples and a pan of cracked walnuts appeared. Sometimes we all played "flinch," a game permitted to Methodists because the cards were built up in order to Thirteen, eliminating the wicked suit-spots and aces-kings-queens-jacks. Sometimes Father read to us while Mother mended or made buttonholes. He read well and with considerable drama. Sometimes, as the children grew older, we took turns reading and were coached into expressiveness.

One final element in the setting is worthy of mention, for it was very different from the one experienced by other children in the neighborhood or even by my sisters. It was the small collection of books which were waiting for me when I could use them. Mother would never tell me when I began

[67]

to read, but it must have been fairly early because by the end of my second day in school I was "in the third reader," and within a few more days had sailed through it to the fourth. Even before that, every morning of my life, except when parked with the Halls, I had listened to the sonorous cadences of the King James Bible. Father followed in his father's footsteps and guests or hands or anybody who happened to be around heard the morning chapter. By the time I was ten I knew the Bible and all its people. The prayers which followed the reading might slip past my negligent ears, but the stories of Noah, Moses, David and all the other characters in the great cast were part of me forever.

When or how Father began to put together his little book collection I shall never know. I wasn't smart enough to ask him. But it was there, waiting for me. To this day I can recall the look and feel of that small shelf of books housed in an old "commode." *Pilgrim's Progress,* in a brown cover and sparked by terrifyingly realistic engravings of Christian and his various troubles. *Paradise Lost,* fine print, green cover, lines that rolled on and on till I fell asleep over them. *Gulliver's Travels,* which I hadn't the faintest perception was anything but a good story. *David Copperfield,* probably a second-hand copy, for the back was broken, but read and reread until Betsy Trotwood, Uriah Heap and Mr. Micawber were as real to me as the neighbors on the next farm. *Vanity Fair,* describing a life at an opposite pole of existence, but so vividly that years later when I stayed at hotels in Mayfair and Brighton, I had the feeling of coming home. *Don Quixote,* wretched print in a cheap edition, but read delightedly for its tale of a broken-down nag with a romantic name, a totally absurd hero, and a super-sensible groom who alone seemed real to me. *Grant's Memoirs,* very thick and dull, but read because it was print of which there was never enough and because Grandfather said every American ought to read it. *The Inferno,* completely over my head though I tried it several times. The *Plays of Shakespeare,* and oh joy, a birthday present of Lamb's *Tales from Shakespeare,* for use as a pony! *The Autobiography of Peter Cartwright,* an odd bit read again and again for the fun of seeing Peter send his frontier ruffians into the "shakes." *Dombey and Son* failed

[68]

to make much of an impression, but its author's *Child's History of England* was read so often that I ever after carried around with me a fair outline of English history. There was also a collection of Tennyson's poems, an illustrated edition of *Hiawatha,* a copy of Meredith's *Lucille,* and a few others.

In the course of time I had my own books, the Alcotts and *Robinson Crusoe* and the Leatherstocking tales, not to mention the Horatio Algers and Elsie Dinsmores borrowed from neighbor children. But the books I kept coming back to, trying to puzzle out their meaning were those on Father's shelf. If there had been more books in my small world, or if the *Youth's Companion* had come oftener than once a week, I might not have tried so desperately to plow such hard soils.

As I look back to that now misty farm, one of its most vivid features is the amount of work which abounded in it. In those days, and certainly in that neighborhood, no social stigma was attached to the use of child labor. The voracious woodbox, the fear-spiked berry-picking, the tedious horse-powered mill and the vegetable garden were only a beginning. In the heat of late summer afternoons or the cold of winter mornings milk cows had to be brought in from the pasture and taken back to it. That involved riding the cow-pony and so was a fun job, at least for Idylene and me. Then there were the morning and evening milkings, at which girls' hands could become skilled at an early age. Chickens must be fed and their watering dishes kept clean and full. Eggs must be gathered every day and peckings warded off when a silly hen decided to "set" at an unseasonable time.

As soon as the little girls were able to help around the house, the "hired girl" disappeared. We took their place at washing dishes, running the washing machine, ironing, cleaning down the stairway and back porch, pitting cherries, peeling apples and peaches, helping Mother can the scores of Mason jars of various fruits and tomatoes, churning butter, dehusking corn ("ros'n ears," we called it) and making underwear and "sack aprons" on the busy old White sewing machine. Somebody even had to grind the Lion-brand coffee for tomorrow's breakfast. During at least two-thirds of every day the Devil would have had to look hard to find any idle hands around that farm. We were needed and we knew it.

Such was the setting in which we lived and had our being. Recently I drove and walked about those acres and scarcely recognized them. The square white farm house had been "modernized," but was empty, for the land was leased to a neighbor farming on a large scale, as men must now do if they are to farm at all. The big barn and orchard and corrals were long gone. Fields had been thrown together, terraced and contour-plowed. The old rows of "Osage Orange" had been rooted out. The house in which I was born, which served as a storage space long after the larger one was built, had been removed so completely that not even the wonderful doorstep remained. The woodlots had diminished and become parklike. There were no berry patches and no vegetable garden. Strangest of all, the hill which had seemed so enormous had flattened to insignificance.

Gone, all gone. No child will ever again grow up in such a setting.

postscripta, 1975

It is one of the minor ironies of my long life that a city-born-and-bred niece now wants above all things to own and operate "a real farm." She is not dreaming of a mechanized agribusiness layout, but a small place where she can grow her own organic food and "keep out of the rat race." My mother's granddaughter!

* * * *

Another irony is that I should have lived to see a machine cut grass and lay it in windrows, then another machine, a very big and lumbering metal container pulled by an air-conditioned tractor, straddle the windrow, suck up the hay, pack it into the big container and finally when the space will hold no more, eject the hay into a beautifully shaped and waterproof small *hay stack.* (Like a hen laying an egg.) In my day a mowing machine cut the hay after the blades had been sharpened on a foot pedaled grindstone; a rake put it into windrows; strong, human arms lifted it into a hayrack; more arms pitched it off the rack; and still more "stacked" it in such a way that moisture could not damage it. All of the operations had to be done by sweating, hard-muscled men, except for raking the cut grass into windrows. That was a job for a sedate horse and a sun-bonnetted little girl.

[70]

4

The School

As I consider the accouterments of today's public schools, no one will believe Belknap. In fact, I don't quite believe it myself.

Education is now a giant industry, a prime political issue, a rich field for "research and development" by publishers and Doctors of Education, an arena wherein embattled taxpayers and professional educators contend, a mill through which children are run with the aim of making them citizens and safe drivers able to cope with the twentieth century, an enormous babysitting service for keeping the young off the streets and the labor market, an instrument for the acculturization of deprived segments of the population, a producer of reliable workers and pliable consumers for the industrial establishment, and occasionally a place of initiation into the life of the intellect.

[71]

With all these functions any proper public school system must employ a multitude of workers: administrators and supervisors, classroom teachers and aides, counselors and coaches, cooks, bus drivers, statisticians, a public relation expert to help out at bond-voting or tax-raising times, secretaries, nurses, maintenance workers whose dignity is underwritten by numerous unions, and heaven knows how many other varieties of work people.

Equipment is limited only by the wealth of the district and the stubborness of taxpayers, but any respectable system will provide twelve years of instruction in pleasant, well-lighted, evenly heated, fireproof rooms. Its lower schools will have good play yards and equipment, an auditorium, and some kind of a library. Upper grades will also possess a grand piano and fairly good stage facilities in the auditorium, a playing field and a gym, a variety of team uniforms, a set of band instruments and uniforms. Even a small system must make at least a stab at vocational training. The smaller it is the more likely is it to have a fleet of buses. It can hardly be so small as to lack typewriters, duplicators, audio-visual machines and an inter-com system which to many teachers seems to function incessantly.

The size of the system is a prime subject for public worry. Bigness is generally conceded to be a Problem, but unless the system can turn out a high school graduation class of at least one hundred, the experts consider it too small to be allowed to exist.

For me and *most* of my contemporaries "school" was one bare room. Before we all die off one of us should try to resurrect the Belknaps of the land before they succumb to rural consolidation and are carted off to serve as farm storage or extra living space.

My first term, the standard six months, was spent in a school very near the Dungan grandparents. I do not even remember the name of the district, but the school itself was a carbon copy of Belknap, as were all the rural schools of that part of the world. Almost my only memory of it is of being the target for that worst of all playground gibes, "Teacher's Pet." It wasn't fair, I told myself hotly, for Grandmother to get me into this trouble by rooming and boarding Teacher.

Absolutely nothing from the first three months of the second term has stayed with me, for that was the year of the Big Pneumonia.

At the beginning of my third year and Hildred's first we went to Belknap. The distance was two and a half miles at a time when that was a good half-hour's drive and school buses weren't even a wild-eyed dream. We were wonderfully lucky, our parents thought, because the school teacher would be driving along the main road down the lane from our house and consented to pick us up, *if* we were there waiting for her.

She was the only teacher I ever heartily disliked. What she was really like there is, of course, no way for me to know. She may have been, as Father thought, a whizz at drilling in grammar rules and multiplication tables. But my eight-year-old self regarded her as a hard, unsmiling old maid who was no friend of children. If Hildred and I were a minute late she scolded mercilessly. I never talked back. All my training forbade that. But when I discovered that my nicest smile and most beguiling line of chatter could not mollify her, I thought, "You're a mean, cranky old woman and I despise you," and then thought about something else until the lecture ran its course. Poor Hildred on the other hand was so distressed that she went into fuming agitation each morning trying to insure that we would be waiting at the corner when Miss Bonafiel's horse and buggy came clattering across the bridge. For the rest of her life Hildred would be punctual though the stars fell. Eventually she raised so much ruckus about the morning behavior of sleepyhead sisters that Father gave her a pony and told her to go on whenever she was ready.

I know now that Miss Bonafiel had no reason to be bright and smiling about either her job or the creatures for whose tutelage it was designed. When we reached the school house, after what must have been for her a two-hour drive through frequently bitter weather, she had to shake down the pot-bellied stove, arrange some kindling, bring out the kerosene from its hiding place, and presently begin to feed in coal. About the time the room was warm the other pupils would come stamping in with their "dinner buckets" and heavy wraps. If it was snowing or raining, the stench from the steaming garments would affront her nostrils. After seven hours of constant alertness, as combined policeman and instructor, she would wash off the blackboard, sweep the floors, bank the fire, and set off again in her buggy.

There were usually about thirty of us, ranging from first-graders, who might be only five, if they took it into their heads to go to school with older brothers and sisters, up to young people about ready to get married. As learners they ranged from me at one end of the spectrum, dying for learning and experience, to a taciturn seventeen-year-old coming because he had nothing else to do during the winter months. For coping with that stove and motley set of younglings, the poor woman was paid thirty-five dollars for each month of the term. Extra good pay, too, because of her reputation as an especially good teacher.

Belknap was not of the "little red" variety, but a white frame box with four bare windows on the north and another four on the south. The September sun could pour in without let or shutter. The whole length of the back wall was covered by a blackboard low enough for the smallest pupil and high enough for the tallest — quite a lot of surface for Teacher to clean at night. To this blackboard we all went to demonstrate our ability to write, "cipher," and diagram sentences.

In the middle of the room, just in front of the blackboard was "teacher's desk," a good-sized unvarnished table with a drawer and a battered straight chair. Along the wall at one side of the desk was our lavatory, a small table on which rested an enamelled wash basin and the water bucket, filled from the cistern just outside and equipped with *one* long-handled tin dipper. Mother provided us with our own cups and nagged us to use them, but that would have set us too sharply apart from our mates. Teacher, however, did maintain a separate drinking cup. Also on the north wall, cornering up to the blackboard and the "lavatory" was the library, a small bookcase with some Dinsmores, Algers, Alcotts, and a Leatherstocking or two. Next to it, in the very center of the room, was the stove, that black monster which either scorched the unfortunate near it or froze the unfortunate in far corners.

Four rows of desks and a row of pegs fanning out from

each side of the door completed the furniture. The desks were each equipped with an inkwell which could be put to all sorts of evil uses; a set of dog-eared textbooks bought by parents and passed down through the family until they no longer held together; a penholder with a steel point which we were instructed to dry off carefully on a scrap of fabric known as a pen-wiper, but which, nevertheless was soon cantankerous from rust; and a slate with an accompanying cleaning rag and a stone pencil which could be made to creak wickedly against the writing surface. These were indeed *slates,* thin slabs of shale framed in wood. They were great conservers of paper because sums done on them could be washed off with a damp sponge or, more likely, a rag brought from home for that purpose. But why bother to go to the water bucket and dribble a little water over sponge or cloth when Nature had provided a good source of moisture in one's mouth?

The desks varied in size from small ones for first-graders in front of Teacher's desk to the big ones designed for full grown adults. All had been embellished by jack knives, which boys carried as soon as they wore pants — considerably later than you may think, but an accomplished fact of life by the first grade. Teacher waged a constant warfare on the carvers, but who could keep an eye on what went on behind every propped book, and once the deed was accomplished, punishment would not restore the desk. The initials and the linked hearts, some of them put there by parents of the artists, made for a troublesome writing surface.

Most of the desk's were "double," wide enough for two. This space-saving device added to Teacher's problems, for when did two children ever sit in proximity without doubling their opportunities for merriment and distraction. Chums always put up a great plea to sit together and had to be separated within a week.

In the two rear corners of the school yard were the outhouses to which pupils asked permission to repair on necessity or to escape an irksome assignment for a few minutes. Occasionally, early in the term, one of the infants in the front row would misjudge his need and not ask in time. The resultant trickle was abject humiliation to him and his older

[75]

brothers and sisters, acute annoyance to the teacher, and tittering enjoyment to everyone else. If Teacher surmised that a request from one of the older students stemmed from boredom rather than nature, she might refuse, and sometimes the refusal was followed by a vengeful odor, which also gave rise to tittering and perhaps nose-holding.

For quite a while after Hallowe'en one year, the hinges on Hers were useless, giving cause for much giggling among occupants and the bang of an occasional snowball or rock on the door — just to let us know that *they* knew its state. Hallowe'en made it possible to fix the date when the hinges became loose and we either snickered or fumed, depending on the stage of our attitude toward Boys. As soon as Father heard about the matter, the hinges were replaced.

The millions who have laughed at the administrative absurdities and cruelties presented in *Up The Down Staircase* and the sentimentalists who mourn the "lack of individual attention in today's regimented public schools," should know what it was like back in those halcyon days when teachers were supposed to have been *teachers,* half way between God and loving parents. Then, as now, the classroom was no place for weaklings, but then, and not now, the classroom teacher was loaded with custodial duties and responsible for protecting the building.

During my five years at Belknap I had three teachers, Miss Bonafiel and two young men. I doubt if any of them had ever seen the inside of a high school building, but they had been to Normal, knew the Three R's and what the textbooks said about history and geography, and could "keep order" without fussing about it. They were amply equipped for the job at hand. The fabled recalcitrance of Big Boys in the frontier school was long gone, but Teacher was no freer from police duties than his charming young successor in Home Room 304. Furthermore he was strictly on his own — there was no principal's office to deal with transgressors. I never saw corporal punishment administered, though a few times I saw a teacher at the end of his rope grasp a pair of shoulders and, in the playground vernacular, "shake him till his teeth rattled." Otherwise, the penalty for untoward behavior was either "staying in" at recess or after school or "standing on

[76]

the floor" (standing, book in hand, beside Teacher's desk or sometimes in a corner) for an unspecified time. It seems to be the fate of elementary teachers of whatever point in history never to be able to relax while on duty.

To this necessity to be constantly on the alert must be added the exigencies imposed by the clock. Usually Teacher had before him eight grades, each of which must receive its own level of instruction in each of the Three R's. The upper grades had also to be instructed in grammar, geography, physiology, and both American and Kansas history. During the last year came a wearisome thing known as "civics," taught by rote, because how else could it be taught in a neighborhood where even the courthouse was nothing but a word to children and most homes hadn't even a newspaper. On an occasional year Teacher would be blessed with the absence of one grade or a situation where he could combine instruction in, say, reading. But mostly he had to cope with eight grades.

School "took up" at nine, "let out" at four. Count out two twenty minute *recesses* (accent on the first syllable, please) and an hour at noon for gobbling the contents of "dinner buckets" with all possible speed and playing every possible minute, and it is easy to calculate that there was never as much as ten minutes for any particular class. When Teacher called for fifth grade reading, several children slid out from under their desks and went to the "recitation bench," there to drone through the assigned pages while the rest of us were supposedly going on with our own work. When the time allotted to them ran out, they had to be sent back to their seats so that another class could come to the bench or be sent to the blackboard.

The much-criticized lock step of today's classroom is no more rigid than Belknap's. If a child failed to march along with his group, the severe time limits imposed by the program allowed Teacher two choices: he could put the flounderer back a grade, which sometimes was very impolitic, especially if the child happened to belong to a school board member, or Teacher could invite him to stay in at noon or awhile after school for special help. Naturally, no pupil wanted *that!* And from the overburdened teacher's standpoint, why should he bother to insist that the straggler stay after school? These children were going to be farmers. In that era it meant they were educationally ready if they were able to add and substract, multiply and divide, write a legible hand, and stumble through the pages of the county newspaper. If a young Belknaper got stuck somewhere, he probably remained so for life — much as his counterpart in one of the poorer schools of today.

For me everything came easy, too easy, alas, in arithmetic. I could memorize a formula and apply it patly to a problem, but never had any notion of what mathematics is all about. The mystery is that nobody, not even the trigonometry teacher who completed my mathematical tutelage, ever caught me and nailed me down to comprehension of the basics.

The easy stuff in my "reader" was soon gulped and the sums soon laid out. Then I was ready to listen to the older students "recite." By the time I got to geography or history, I already knew what was in the textbooks. Since Teacher was in no way able to amplify their contents, all my later years afforded more boredom than enlightenment.

The only time in the entire week when I was fully engaged was the last period on Friday when we had a spelling or a "ciphering" match. The student I have mentioned as coming for lack of anything else to do was magnificently indifferent to grammar, history or geography. Fully grown and so silent as to seem sullen, he was one of the "big boys" who sometimes at noon drifted out of the school yard to a nearby hedge row to have a smoke and a game of pitch or poker with the greasy deck he carried along with pipe and knife. But he came to life during those late Friday afternoon sessions.

The ciphering Fridays didn't much concern me, because I lost too often. I could get up and down columns of figures fast enough but had trouble herding them into the right fold. I was quick at multiplication and long division, but every now and then tripped up on a seven-times. But not Bill. He would half crouch, with one foot braced against the blackboard wall and the other well back, his eyes like slits, his eraser hand poised as his chalk hand moved up one column and down the next. He wasn't terribly fast, but if and when he made a mistake, that was a day to remember.

[78]

Spelling Fridays were another batch of cookies. The whole school participated, but the smaller children were soon "out." Then Teacher turned a few pages to harder words. When only Bill and I were left, Teacher flipped to the back of the spelling book and the whole room became quiet and intensely partisan. Only my sisters, a young cousin, and a few of the other small fry were saddened on the days when I lost.

It is a mark of the esteem in which spelling was then held that these matches consumed the whole last period of Friday. Both Bill and I took to studying the back pages of the "speller" as preparation. No doubt his life has been as little troubled as mine by stumpers like "harass" and "embarrass."

On the playground, particularly in the later years, I was nobody's darling. What my Southern grandmother daintily called my "limbs" were too short for running. I couldn't catch or bat, often couldn't even get the ball over the roof in Andy Over. I wasn't much at easy rope-jumping, and just nothing at all when "hot pepper" began to be poured on. So I was never chosen until far down the list, no matter what the game. I was small for my age and after my illness Mother kept my hair bobbed so that I looked even more juvenile than I was. Naturally I resented my place in the social order. I felt it beneath my dignity to play with the younger children and my classmates wouldn't have *me*. The more they rejected me on the playground, the more satisfaction I got when they had scholastic difficulties. And when I tripped up in class, how pleased they were! In school I was a real outsider, never allowed to forget it and forever assuring myself that I really didn't mind.

There were, of course, other exciting times than Friday afternoons.

The Thanksgiving program, for instance. Christmas and Memorial Day (which we called Decoration Day) belonged to the church. Thanksgiving went to the school. Parents came in at mid-afternoon Wednesday to hear us speak "pieces" they and Teacher had been drilling into us. Because some one had once raised money to buy dark green cotton for "curtains" to string on a wire extended across the front of the room, we could create some suspense for ourselves if not

[79]

the audience by closing the curtains while we set the stage for the playlet, called a "dialog," which capped our show. Although the day of pumpkin-and-turkey paper artwork was far in the future, Teacher usually managed to display some pictures of the Pilgrim Fathers going to the first Thanksgiving with their guns over their shoulders.

But the biggest day was Last Day of School. Then parents came in at noon with baskets of chicken, potato salad, pie and cake. For a day or two Teacher would be upset because some of us hadn't settled down to learn our pieces well enough to let him feel easy. He also had reasonable grounds for fearing that some one, or several some ones, would bobble in "the dialogs." If we put on an exhibition in ciphering or spelling, it was important to him that he seem to have done well with us — and those final days were blasted with mistakes. We ourselves were keyed up by the responsibilities laid on us as well as by the months of freedom ahead.

Finally it arrived, and with it a last morning of coaching and drilling. Our anxious watching of the road to spot the first arrivals naturally interfered with our concentration until Teacher was, "fit to be tied, poor soul." Just before noon parents began to arrive, waiting in their carriages or buggies until Teacher let us out, whooping, at the stroke of noon.

Then what visiting and "joshing" in the crowded room on this fiesta for the neighborhood! How they all crammed into the little school building I cannot understand, but somehow they all did, and somehow the boxes or baskets of food were spread out on the desks. When the meal was over and the women had cleared away the debris, the program began, littlest performers first, each parent waiting for his own sprout to distinguish himself, and all applauding every performer heartily so as to assure a good hand for you know who.

"Last Day" was a great day, ranking with Decoration Day and just under Christmas. In family custom and festivals we had, of course, Thanksgiving, the day when, under the ministrations of Grandmother H in her best white apron with its wide lace border, the Bird made his once-a-year ritual appearance before a tableful of adult relatives and heaven knows how many cousins. Mother never cooked a turkey until her mother was no longer able to stand before the oven, and the other grandmother never ventured into that field of competition. Christmas was another day of relatives and quivering nostrils while a goose or two were roasting, but much more importantly, a day of Presents. Labor Day was unknown, and if it had been a holiday would have seemed a sinful waste of a perfectly good Monday. Fourth of July was chancy. If the weather was normal for Kansas — that is, perverse — the corn was at a critical stage where every day out of the fields could be costly.

Only if it was a "good year," when planting had been early, rains had come and corn was "laid by" — that is, past the need for cultivation and ready to cope with weeds on its own — was the neighborhood able to celebrate. Perhaps because this gala occasion was so uncertain and because when it came adults were always in such good spirits, I remember it as topping even Christmas, Presents notwithstanding.

A few days before the Fourth on those blessed years when the weather behaved, father and some of the other men cleared out the weeds and undergrowth in a woodlot and the neighborhood got itself ready for a rousing picnic. It was a great time for everyone. For children firecrackers and pop were on hand, and for sale. For young people of courting age it was a rare chance to be together in the day time, and for farmers and their wives it was a chance to see each other when everybody was in an expansive mood because this year, Glory be, the corn crop looked promising.

In every house on such a morning there was near bedlam among the young. About eleven we all began to convene, in carriages, buggies or, if the family had committed itself to bring sawhorses and planks for the tables, in wagons. The horses were tied out on the rim of the grove, as far away from the firecracker stand as possible. Lemons were squeezed in the same great earthenware crocks in which, come August and the peak of the cabbage crop, sauerkraut would be made. Lemonade would be cooled with a block of ice brought by some one, usually the Dungans. The wooden ice cream freezers that children had painfully turned and fathers had carefully "packed" were stored in the shade and carefully covered with old comforters. Tables were assembled and covered with oil cloth or checked cotton table cloths. Paper

[81]

napkins were far in the future, but every experienced mother had brought along towels. and washclothes to mop off their grubby sprigs before and after. Then the food was laid out, mountains of fried chicken and potato salad, coleslaw by the gallon, devilled eggs, great bowls of baked beans, pickles and jams in every variety, a daunting assortment of pies and of cakes to be eaten with the ice cream.

As long as the fireworks and soda pop lasted, they were where our money was spent. As long as it lasted children had the delicious agony of deciding how to apportion out their acquired wealth. We usually had better than a dollar apiece, earned in that hateful blackberry patch at the rate of ten cents and twenty-five chigger bites a gallon. Idylene's and my money was soon gone, but Hildred had to consider so carefully how she would spend hers that the items for sale disappeared before her money gave out, so she was able to take home a good part of hers.

At mid-afternoon, when the firecrackers had banged out, sparklers had fizzed out and stomachs were sluggish from the onslaughts to which they had been subjected, our speaker got up to remind us of the grand and glorious event we were celebrating. If it was an even-numbered year he would likely be a candidate for a county office. In odd numbered years he might be a lawyer out from the county seat looking for future clients or a minister out from Moline with his family for a day's outing and country eating. When the "speaking" was over, women began to "gather up" and men to "put the horses to." With many goodbyes each family went home to do its chores: gather the eggs, milk the cows and feed the pigs. Children, exhausted by all the excitements of the day, were usually asleep before a half mile had passed, lucky if they did not wake up afire with chigger bites.

*   *   *   *

At that point in the history of Kansas education the county superintendents had a rite known as County Eighth Grade Examinations, which was, I think, the sole standardized achievement test in the whole state system. I took the test four months before my twelfth birthday and passed.

While going through some old papers recently, I ran onto

the questions which qualified me for my eighth grade diploma. The questions on that examination in that primitive, one-room school taught by a young person who never attended a high school positively daze me.

The "orthography" quiz ("Heavens," I thought as I looked at the little piece of brittle paper, "what does that word mean?") asked us to spell twenty words, including "abbreviated," "obscene," "elucidation," "assassination" and "animosity." We were also required to "make a table" showing the different sounds of all the vowels with *oo, g, c,* and *s* thrown in for good measure. Among the other eight questions (each subject had ten questions) was one which asked us to "divide into syllables and mark diacritically the words "profuse, retrieve, rigidity, defiance, priority, remittance, and propagate."

Two of arithmetic's ten questions asked us to find the interest on an eight-per-cent note for $900 running 2 years, 2 months, 6 days; and also to reduce 3 pecks, 5 quarts, 1 pint to bushels. In Reading we were required to tell what we knew of the writings of Thomas Jefferson, and for another of the ten questions to "indicate the pronunciation and give the meanings of the following words: Zenith, deviated, coliseum, misconception, panegyric, Spartan, talisman, eyrie, triton, crypt. (What a line-up for a Belknap, or any other country child of the period!)

Among Geography's ten were these two: "Name two countries producing large quantities of wheat; two of cotton, two of coal, two of tea." "Name three important rivers of the U.S.; three of Europe, three of Asia, three of South America, and three of Africa."

As one of Physiology's ten we were, young Kansans that we were, asked to "write 200 words on the evil effects of alcoholic beverages!" Another directed us to define Boards of Health and tell what their duties were.

In grammar's ten were two directing us to "analyze and diagram": "There is a tide in the affairs of men, which taken at the flood, leads on to fortune." And then to *parse* (the meaning of which I am now a little hazy about) *tide, which, taken, leads.*

In history we were to "give a brief account of the colleges,

[83]

printing, and religion in the colonies prior to the American Revolution," to "name the principal campaigns and military leaders of the Civil War," to "name the principal political questions which have been advocated since the Civil War and the party which advocated each."

Looking at those yellowed lists of questions taught under the conditions which prevailed at all the Belknaps in the land, I am somewhat awed. I passed them then, but I would have a hard time with them now. Rote memory was what it took in 1907, but fortunately mine was better then than now.

When my family took me on an overnight trip to the county seat (twenty miles away!) the evening ceremony of diploma-bestowal seemed to me a blaze of lights and glory. The attention I received because of my size and age in comparison with the other graduates inflated my ego perilously.

Until that time I had been puzzled when my classmates at times couldn't seem to understand what was perfectly simple. Now I began to suspect that my "difference" might be something to preen myself on. Because a "swell head" was about the worst thing one could be in the eyes of contemporaries, I had carefully refrained from labelling or even examining my difference. But, I began to accept it. During the next year I must have been insufferable in spite of all my prayers to be made "nice."

The eighth grade graduation posed a problem for my parents. Twelve years was entirely too young for sending a child away to school and, besides, physically, I wasn't even a decent twelve-year-old. Consequently, they sent me back to Belknap for another year, kept me at music lessons, and tried to provide me with more books. That year I learned absolutely nothing in school. Much later, when I was being hard-driven in the University of Illinois graduate school, I used to look back to that last term at Belknap and long for some of the hours diddled away in dreams of the day when I would be rich and famous and "they" (my parents) would be so proud of my accomplishments that they would lavish love and praise upon me and never, never require me to do anything disagreeable.

But the thirteenth birthday eventually came, bringing another decision. There were no school buses anywhere in the land traveling up and down highways collecting farm children and delivering them back in the late afternoon. If a youngster went on to high school, he had to board and room or do "light housekeeping" with a family in town for the five school days. When it came Hildred's and Idylene's turn they did just that. But the little high school in Moline wasn't much and the Grandparents Dungan now lived just off the campus of a small Methodist college, which at that time had an "academy" to prepare rural youngsters for college. As I look back to it, and think of the times, it must have been a pretty good preparatory school. It consisted of around seventy students altogether. It was excessively pious in atmosphere because most of us were either from "good Methodist homes" which purposed us to grow up good Methodists or men already in their twenties trying to get ready for college so as to prepare for a Methodist ministry. But we had good teachers, most of whom taught at least a class or two in college. Three of them I remember as excellent. And, joy of joys, we had free and unlimited access to the college library! It wasn't much of a library even then and nothing by today's library standards, but to me it was riches unlimited. By the time I left the school with an A.B. I had ploughed through a good share of everything in the stacks, except the mathematical and philosophic books. I have always blessed my parents for giving me up at age thirteen. To do it they must have been moved by an immense faith in the necessity for education.

While I learned nothing scholastically that last year at Belknap, I had an experience eminently worth it all. I fell in love with a boy named Charlie, whom Father defamed as a "little Pop" because his father had been an enthusiastic Populist during that political uproar. I kept strictly to myself the delicious new feelings I was having — nothing could have dragged them out of me. But an old novel reader, such as I was, could easily identify them. So *this*, I told myself wonderingly, was how all those heroines felt!

Unfortunately, Charlie liked Eva instead of me, and that was to be my fate for several years. The boys I liked couldn't see me. The ones who showed signs of interest in me were practically nauseating. All except one — and if he didn't set me a-quiver emotionally, he had some tremendous points.

[85]

He was in my class at the academy and like me was "ahead of himself." He was still wearing short pants in our first year. But his father was president of the town's First National Bank and owned a Buick which Junior drove whenever he could get his hands on it, and that was often. Because nobody in our class wanted any social contact with its two babies, we were thrown together at all parties and wiener roasts. But that beautiful, hand-cranked, brass-trimmed, lordly-voiced Buick gave us a standing we could never have earned for ourselves.

postscriptum, 1975

In my St. Louis neighborhood we have a large public school with "special rooms" for children with "learning difficulties," a small public school for kindergarten through third grade, a good-sized parochial school, an "alternative school," and a "neighborhood school." Both the public and the parochial systems have high schools. No teacher has less than an A.B., most of them Masters degrees. And yet employers and university professors are saying that many high school graduates can neither spell, put together three decent sentences, nor do anything but the simplest of arithmetic.

Percentage-wise, the students who learned what they needed to know in order to function well on the scene where *chance* dropped them is undoubtedly lower than it was back in Belknap.

<h1 style="text-align:center">5</h1>

The Church

For better than forty years I have belonged to one or another large urban church with carpeted aisles, comfortable pews, robed choir and ritualized service, many classrooms, budget in six figures, and an eloquent, well-educated minister. In addition, there has been a full range of assistant ministers, office staff, custodians, boards and commissions, and teacher-training institutes directed by professionals in religious education. In all these churches there has been at least a "saving remnant" of members who have thought of the church's mission in wider terms than their own individual salvation and the induction of their young into the faith of their fathers.

Even today such churches are a long way from those in rural America. The distance from a Belknap of the century's first decade is practically astronomical.

Except for the family at the turn of the century, church and school constituted the entire institutional life of a neighborhood. We were much more isolated and self-contained than any American neighborhood can be in the age of electronics. One or the other of those two white, oblong boxes furnished the setting for almost the whole social life of everybody. The only exception were young people of courting age. If they were Methodist they went to "play parties," otherwise to godless dances where a bottle was sometimes passed around. Even this extra-mural social life was brief. Almost as soon as they married and certainly as soon as the wife was noticeably pregnant, it was considered proper for them to put away such juvenile pleasures. In either the church or the school was centered almost every phase of the neighborhood social life other than courting, then irreverently known as "sparking" even though a lot of that went on in the two frame buildings.

Other rural institutions were not yet in existence, or had not reached Belknap. There were no cooperatives, no Four H Clubs, no Farm Bureau, no political clubs. After the Populist fires died down, Kansans settled comfortably back into the Grand Old Party. Moreover there was no cultural or social linkage with the nearest town. A farm woman several horse-and-buggy miles from town was not likely to take it into her head to join one of the women's clubs just beginning to be organized in small-town America. Even had such a notion occurred to her she would have been too shy to pursue it, and probably wouldn't have been welcomed if she had. In those days a great gulf was fixed between town and coutry. Some of the men did belong to the Oddfellows, perhaps for the insurance. But the trip home from a meeting was so long after a day in the fields and bedtime so late before another day in the fields that men rarely went to the meetings. People in places like Belknap either made their own social life or they would have none.

By the time I was leaving Belknap the school term had been extended to seven months. But, except for an occasional box supper or "literary," adults came to the school for the Thanksgiving and Last Day programs. Church, of course, went on the year around. So everybody, sinner and saint, true believer and unbeliever, went to it. Nowhere else could he see his neighbors regularly. Whoever habitually stayed away from Sunday morning "preaching" was at least partly separating himself from his community. *Nobody* at all stayed away from the funerals, the Christmas trees and box suppers in winter and the strawberry-and-cream or ice-cream-and-cake money-raising suppers in summer. Some quirk in the neighborhood mores decreed that weddings be held in the bride's home or, in unfortunate cases when Papa was being unreasonable, at the office of the Justice of Peace. Every other social function, except the occasional Fourth of July celebration, was centered in school or church.

Each year of my childhood there was a Memorial Day service at which children (trained by Mother) stepped through a flag drill, several of us spoke patriotic "pieces," everybody sang *America* and some one read the *Gettysburg Address*. After that we all went to the cemetery behind the school yard. At its entrance we fell into a little procession with the remaining "old soldiers" of the Civil War at our head. Uncle Dick Speed, a spry little fellow who had joined the Union Army as a drummer boy at age fourteen, gave us a flourish or two and then drummed us down into the cemetery, where commemorative shots were fired over the graves of departed veterans, and people paused to put flowers on the graves of their own dead. After that came the "visiting," the real reason, of course, for every meeting held in either school or church.

But when Grandfather was organizing the "class" at Belknap and trying to get mission funds for construction, he wasn't thinking of any community center. What he had in mind was a House of God. And the ministers who shouted from the pulpit as they warmed to the theme of the day were aiming only to strengthen the faithful and stir the unregenerate to repentance. As in every other church, the intended function was religious instruction. For most people the actual function was a mix in which religion was not the prime ingredient.

Since so few people now living have experienced the rural Methodism of that time, something should be explained about

[89]

its structure. It was a firmly organized episcopal system, running down from the bishops presiding over "conferences," through "presiding elders" in charge of "districts," to ordained ministers assigned by their superiors to specified "charges" (parishes), to local preachers who functioned as their own fervor and the exigencies of their surroundings dictated. Grandfather was a local preacher.

Belknap was one of three rural churches linked together in a "circuit," served by one preacher. Belknap was our Preacher's first service. That meant he either came into the neighborhood on Saturday to do some pastoral work or he must get up very early in order to drive the twelve miles from the hamlet where the parsonage was located.

If he came on Saturday, it could be guaranteed he would stay at the Dungans. In the early years, when the babies were coming and Mother was often ill, he ate Grandmother's fried chicken and slept between sheets she had washed on a board and then smoothed with a flat iron that had been heated on a hot stove.

Later, when the Dungans Senior moved away, he stayed with us. Since his presence meant some inconvenience for the daughters of the household, they prepared for his arrival late Saturday afternoon with considerably less than enthusiasm. Moreover, they saw him as a dampener of spirits and a spouter of obscure theological views. In short, a much less interesting guest than "the Baker man" who came regularly into the neighborhood with a cart load of spices and liniments and who laid himself out to be entertaining. (Among his other narrative accomplishments, he could give a rendition of the Crooked Mouthed Family which never failed to convulse us.)

Looking back, the little girls were justified in their reactions. Our preachers were not people to whom hearts went out easily. The reason was that churches like Belknap were at the bottom of the Methodist totem pole. Its ministers were either older men who had failed to make it up the pole or youngsters trying to get started. In my early days it was our luck to have the older men, those who couldn't be sent to a "better" charge. They would stay with us for a year or two, then be moved on to another Belknap. Later on, we once had a "student preacher," who was not only young and unmarried, but of untheological demeanor. For **him** the extra baking was no bother whatever. For him we gladly put an extra polish on the house.

I know now that the older men, toward whom the females of our household felt so snooty, were not going to heaven on any flowery beds of ease. After one of them had finished delivering a forty to sixty minute sermon to us, he had to get into his buggy, eat the box lunch his wife or Grandmother or Mother had packed for him, drive five or six miles to a "class" which met in a school house, preach another sermon, then drive on to the church beside the parsonage for yet another sermon. Three services and up to twenty-four miles in a buggy weren't exactly calculated to get the best from any man. Furthermore, he was not even a high school graduate, certainly had not seen the inside of a seminary. Whatever library he possessed was likely to be "religious books," so doctrinal that in order to read them at all he had to be afire with zeal for saving souls. And beyond all that, his salary was not only microscopic but nearly always in arrears. Many farmers thought they were being generous when they gave him a ham at butchering time or loaded his buggy with surplus eggs and roasting ears in July.

By the time one of these older men arrived in Belknap he had lost any hope of moving up the pole. What, then, motivated him to the work? The cynic might say, with Mother and Grandmother in their darker moods, that he liked a job in which he could wear a white shirt and have people look up to him. Any one who has relished the experience of speaking to an audience that is obliged to maintain at least an air of respectful attention knows that those three Sunday hours in the pulpit must have been balm to an ego which had to endure a good deal of laceration.

But the cynics were only partly right. These men regarded themselves as the agents of God, their words as His words. If they had to thunder from a make-do pulpit to the dull ears of squirming children and half-awake farmers, did not Elijah do so before them?

Entrance to the church was, of course, from the end nearest the road. Across the room were set eight or ten rows of "pews," long wooden seats painted gray, each with a six-inch cross

[91]

Lonely Farmhouse

board arranged for the support of adult backs, but not right for young backs, particularly when the legs that went with the backs were dangling inches above the floor. On the north side of the room, about midway between front and back, was the stove, identical in looks and temperament to its twin in the schoolhouse. In one corner of the room was a reed organ, half-surrounded by what we called "the choir seats." In a line with the organ was the pulpit, an upright box of golden oak, which cost several pie suppers when it replaced a small square table. In front of the pulpit and organ was a rail where members could partake of Communion when the presiding elder came on his quarterly rounds, or where sinners and backsliders might gather at revival time.

The windows were bare and somewhat bleary. Against them in summer bumped an occasional grasshopper. Through them came the sad murmur of crickets and katydids in autumn or the creature silence of winter. The hymn books were a battered old collection of what are nowadays somewhat disdainfully known as "gospel hymns."

It was what seemed an absolutely endless drive from home to church. But during the five or six months when school was out, our need for change from the week's routine and a chance to see other children was so desperate that this ride and what beckoned from the end of it was the high point of the week. I never fully understood the depth of our need for stimulation until a few years ago when I heard an Irish bus driver and yarn-spinner describe his childhood in an isolated village whose repetitious routines set up in him such a longing for something, for *anything* to happen that even funerals were intensely welcome because they generated wakes. Belknap children never heard of wakes, but we certainly looked forward to Sundays.

From the minute when the horses were hitched to the posts, our faces took on a special look reserved for Sunday, the day after the night when we had all been thoroughly scrubbed and our hair washed and put up on kid curlers. As we got out of the carriage, we carefully smoothed out any wrinkles that might have accumulated in our starched white dresses, had our pink or blue sashes adjusted, straightened our straw hats and walked, just as Mother always exhorted, "like little

[93]

ladies," into the church and down to one of the rows of seats toward the front of the room. We never had to be told where to sit. We knew where we belonged, for we were Dungans and from the beginning Dungans, as the church's chief movers and doers, had gravitated toward the front seats. Not the very front; that would have been laying it on too thick. Just near it.

We were in for a long service. First an hour of Sunday School, then preaching at eleven, and after that, during the years when Grandfather was still in the neighborhood, something called a "class meeting." He was very firm about the necessity for it, and as local preacher he could have his way as long as anybody stayed for it. I think now that it must have been a form of compromise for him, a substitute for the prescribed midweek prayer meeting which time had demonstrated Belknapers simply would not attend.

Luckily, Sunday School came first, for at its conclusion we were given copies of The Classmate, a four page publication full of homilies and edifying little stories which could be read during the sermon if we were quiet about it. In this respect Father and Mother were very modern, for children of an earlier generation had been required to sit up straight and at least *look* attentive.

As soon as several families had straggled in, Father went to the front of the room and announced the opening of Sunday School. Some child was asked to pass out the hymnbooks, and whatever young woman was organist went up front, ready to start pedaling when Father gave out the hymn. The songs we sang at Sunday School were of the same character as those at the preaching service and quite different in both sentiment and quality of music from those which now grace the Methodist Hymnal.

One of our favorites was *Bringing in the Sheaves,* though by my time the group had begun to weary of it a little. At least we knew what sheaves were and why it was important that they be brought in — which was more than could be said for another song we Kansans loved to belt out:

"Throw out the Life Line across the dark wave,
   There is a brother whom some one should save;
   Somebody's brother! Oh, who then will dare,

To throw out the Life Line, his peril to share.
Throw out the Life Line with hand quick and strong;
Why do you tarry, why linger so long?
See! He is sinking, oh hasten today,
And out with the Life Boat, away, then away!"
A third great old-timer of ours was:
"Work for the night is coming,
Work through the morning hours,
Work while the dew is sparkling,
Work mid springing flowers.
Work when the day grows brighter,
Work in the glowing sun,
Work for the night is coming, when man's work is done.
Work, for the night is coming,
Work through the sunny noon;
Fill brightest hours with labor,
Rest comes sure and soon.
Give every flying minute
Something to keep in store;
Work, for the night is coming,
    when man works no more."

When I first read the phrase "Protestant work ethic," I remembered that song and audibly laughed right in the middle of the University of Illinois library stacks.

Other favorites were: "What a Friend We Have in Jesus," "God Will Take Care of You" and "Jesus, Lover of my Soul." Unsophisticated tunes, all of them, and easy for the few people with good voices to harmonize. Since we, like most congregations without professional direction, tended to repeat the songs we liked and could sing, no doubt our efforts could be heard a quarter of a mile away even when the windows were closed.

After I began to play the organ at about age eleven, I didn't want Father or the preacher to get too free in the selection of hymns. In spite of Mother's ambitions for me and the considerable amount of practice I did in order to avoid housework and have the place of honor on Sunday, I always needed to "know" a hymn, because I had an unreliable ear and probably the leakiest musical memory ever to plague a girl on that organ stool. If I didn't know a hymn and the congregation could only bumble along with me, it was a most embarrassing situation. No doubt the others in the line of girls before and after me had as little liking for new songs. But I doubt if any of them suffered so much mortification as I did. I may not have been gifted musically, but I had an unsurpassed talent for humiliation by what I considered an inept performance.

After a couple of songs and a short prayer thanking the Lord for bringing us together another week and asking Him to bless our endeavors, the little assembly was broken up into three to five "classes," depending on how many were present and how many teachers had been kept home by a new baby or somebody's earache. Mother, undoubtedly by her own choice, usually had the smallest children, those who couldn't read and probably heard precious few stories at any other time. As everybody knows at least by hearsay, the Bible is full of good stories. Mother was a first-rate storyteller. Also the Methodist publishing house sent out bright colored little picture cards to illustrate the lesson of the day. So at least one class had a thoroughly enjoyable thirty minutes or so.

There was also an adult group, called the Bible Class, taught by the minister if he had come to the neighborhood on Saturday, otherwise by Grandfather as long as he was there and after that by Father. This group used what was known as a "Quarterly" for a text and attempted to discuss the doings of various Biblical characters and the tenets of Christian faith and ethics. Since warm arguments sometimes broke out in the Bible Class, its members must have enjoyed their time together.

For the in-between groups things were not so good. Depending upon the number of children not immured at home by illness and the number of adults whom Father could dragoon into teaching, all the children who could read with some proficiency were divided into one, two, or three groups. In fine weather when there was no epidemic in the neighborhood the teen-agers (not then known by that term because nobody had begun to think of them as a special class of humanity) might be able to assemble by themselves. On very meager days they might find themselves shoved in with eight-year-olds.

In either case the "class lesson" was nothing very exciting to an adolescent. Mostly it consisted of "reading around," one verse to a child, through the Bibical text on which the lesson was grounded. In addition, the "Golden Text" of the day was analyzed and perhaps memorized. After that the group took turns reading, paragraph by paragraph, through the lesson "helps" provided for us by whatever agency was the forerunner of the Methodist Board of Publications. During all this reading each child performed with whatever expertness he could muster. If one of them bumbled, it was no news to him or the rest of us — he also bumbled at school, with the same shriveling of his ego. I, who had heard the lesson and parallel passages read from the King James Version after each breakfast, along with a cumulative explanation of each, was naturally bored. Besides, I wanted to get my hands on The Classmate.

The Golden Text was a short, usually one-sentence, portion of the Bible into which was condensed a bit of the religious heritage which Methodists wanted to be implanted in their children's hearts. "Pride goeth before a fall" and "God so loved the world that he gave his only begotten son so that whosoever believeth on Him shall never die," were typical. "A soft answer turneth away wrath" is another which has stayed with me through the years, though perhaps only because it was such a favorite of Mother's on the numerous occasions when wrath plainly sizzled in her vicinity. During my teen years Grandmother D often pelted me with the one about pride and its consequences.

It was a favorite device of parents to ask their children on the way home to repeat the Golden Text. On one such occasion a small cousin of mine replied, "David went on the blue grass and the Lord got a post after him." Inquiry disclosed that the text had been, "And David went on and grew great and the Lord God of Hosts was with him."

In addition to "reading around" there was a certain amount of checking on our progress in the memorizing we were supposed to be doing in preparation for being taken into membership when and if we became "converted." This memorization was the Belknap equivalent of the confirmation classes which have always been held in Catholic and Episcopal churches and are now a regular part of the urban Protestant program.

The minimum requirement for us was The Lord's Prayer. the Twenty-third Psalm, the Apostles Creed, a listing of the books of the Bible in their order, and the Ten Commandments. It took me quite a while and considerable research through Father's Unabridged Webster to find out what the Seventh really meant. An earlier question had been evaded by some adult. When a child could repeat all of these, he was presented with either a New Testament or a complete Bible in print so fine that he would need much better than 20-20 vision to read it comfortably. But the children of the neighborhood liked having it ceremoniously presented, and perhaps some of them occasionally picked it up and read a bit of it. I myself read at least selected parts of it as a matter of course, partly because of the requirements laid on me as a Dungan and mostly because it was print.

Several times I resolved to read straight through from "In the beginning" right on to the end of Revelation, but I never got far with that. At other times I determined to read a chapter a day, but that resolution also soon evaporated. Not even the scarcity of print could hold me to the letters of St. Paul. Grandfather could quote him by the hour, but I simply couldn't make out what the Saint was talking about, except for a few things like the magnificent chapter on love.

At eleven o'clock Sunday School came to an end, the minister moved up to the pulpit, announced another hymn and Act II was one. By the time I was ten I was either in the choir or on the organ stool, and so had a good view of everybody, from the youngsters who could be trusted to sit by themselves on the front row, right back to the young males in the back row. The youngsters usually fell asleep, but it must have been a rugged hour for the back-seaters. They were drowsy from their life in the open — even Father nodded now and then. In addition, they probably had been out sparking the night before, maybe at some wicked dance with a swig or two of corn whiskey to loosen their muscles for the dancing. The man at the pulpit wasn't saying anything with much connection to life as they lived it. Even in my glow of moral superiority I could see that it was a dull hour for them.

But there was simply nothing else for them to do on a Sunday morning. There was no work after the morning chores. Only in dire straits did a Belknaper put a team into a field on Sunday. Once in a while when rain threatened a quantity of "down" hay, some of them would rush to stack it, but mostly they obeyed the Biblical injunction to rest on the seventh day. Father *never* disobeyed it! There was also for these young men no Sunday paper, no magazines, no movie, no horse or dog race, no ball game, and of course no radio or television — in fact, nothing but church. So they came, Sunday after Sunday, and got through the hour as best they could. Their suffering was mitigated by the presence, down a few rows toward the front, of young females upon whom they had either a hopeful or a possessive eye. And after the service they could keep an eye on Her while swapping yarns and pipe tobacco in the church yard.

Some reminiscers can fish up a remembered sermon to serve as an illustration. I can't. I only remember that the ministers would read a long passage from the Bible, often from St. Paul whose literary style repelled me and whose talk about Old-Man-New-Man baffled me. After the "reading," the minister prayed earnestly and long, in the religious language of the time. It was wholly familiar. Father and Grandfather used it every day, and I never doubted to Whose ears it was being directed. But often when it proceeded from the pulpit, I had the somewhat scary feeling that it was directed "at" the congregation instead of to the unseen God. This feeling troubled me for it might mean that, like Absalom, I was hardening my heart, which I certainly didn't care to do in view of all the consequences predicted for such misbehavior.

At length the minister launched into his sermon. It might go on for an hour if he got carried away with the theme of the day. It was not written out. Heaven forbid! Usually he didn't even have notes. He began to talk on the text he had chosen, trusting the Lord to put words into his mouth. The Lord always did, though sometimes in a rambling flow which gushed faster and louder until its source took a hasty look at the Ingersoll laid out on the pulpit. If the glimpse was reassuring, he plunged back into the stream of words. If not, he brought it to a close.

[99]

What the minister had been saying he believed with his whole mind and heart. His world was much like Job's, one in which God and the Devil walked the earth contending for the loyalty of man. The Devil could make things tough, but in the end God was always stronger if only one gave his life to Him. One who continued to let the Devil hold sway would surely burn in the everlasting fires of Hell. He who was converted and "believed on the Lord Jesus Christ" would go to a blissful afterlife with angel choirs and eternal joy with the loved ones who had preceded him.

"Believe on the Lord Jesus Christ," the minister would shout, "and you shall be saved." Sometimes I would pull myself out of the Classmate and wonder about that. Who **didn't** believe on the Lord Jesus Christ, Son of God and Son of Man? Didn't everybody know that the Bible said He was born of the Virgin Mary, crucified, dead and buried, risen the third day and, some time later, floated back up to Heaven? And if you knew something you believed it, didn't you?

Or he might get started on the theme of salvation from sin, which also puzzled me. I didn't feel very sinful, though I knew I often sneaked off to a book when I was supposed to be working and often made the truth more interesting by a little touching up here and there. But I couldn't seem to feel much guilt for these malefactions — certainly not enough to make reform appear desirable. Which undoubtedly meant that the Protestant ethic which Father and Grandfather totally accepted was being watered down. Hard work and unvarnished truth were not absolute values for me as for them — and alas, never have been.

Idylene claims to have been terrified of burning in hell. I can't remember ever regarding that as a likely prospect for myself. Perhaps I was simply a pint-sized Pharisee. But more likely I had heard too many arguments between Grandfather and Uncle 'Lish about predestination and sanctification. If **they** couldn't agree on matters of such vital importance to them, how could I hope to know for sure? Besides, it was more fun to read *Stepping Heavenward,* the story of a frivolous, quick-tempered young woman's growth into near sainthood.

So I would drift back into the Classmate and when it was

finished, into a dream of the glorious future I was going to have in some vague but very glamorous place — perhaps in a big, exciting city or a fashionable resort by the sea where on a stormy night I would maybe see a lifeline thrown out to a sinking boat. Belknap was not for me. No indeed. Like the magic child in the fairy tales, I had been dropped here, but eventually I would find my way to my rightful place in the universe.

It would be many years before a chance confidence from my mother let me know that I was repeating her childhood fantasy.

When at last the closing hymn was over and the minister had departed to his next sermon, everybody could greet each other and exchange neighborhood news. By this time the Classmate was long finished and my stomach was letting me know that breakfast was also long gone. But until Grandfather moved away, Act III was still ahead. Only the faithful participated in it, but their children had to stay with them, waiting for transportation, and keeping quiet.

The few people who stayed for Act III repeated the same "testimony" Sunday after Sunday. Some of them "blessed God" for the assurance that they were saved. Others related once more the circumstances under which they were converted. Occasionally, some one would describe some heartening experience which had come to him during the past week. I liked that one, for it was something like a story, but on the whole Classmeeting was an affliction for both body and soul.

They prayed for grace to bear the crosses laid upon them and strength to face their disappointments. Sometimes Grandfather ran on a bit about the fear of God being the beginning of wisdom. Once when I was especially hungry and fidgety, and he was especially eloquent, it occurred to me that his firmness about the necessity for this meeting arose from the fact that *he* led it. I brushed that out of my mind in a hurry. Honor thy father — and especially thy tall, saintly, red-bearded Grandfather.

At last, the meeting was over and we were in the carriage going home to the chicken or ham Mother had left in the oven and the pie and cake she had baked the day before. The ride home seemed shorter in spite of my complaining stomach.

[101]

We had been with people and had lifted our voices once more to the vast Presence we had been trained to feel brooding about us.

In spite of all the sitting-still, Sunday was the high day of the week. Even the afternoons were apart from everyday afternoon routines. There was no work! Occasionally a neighbor child came home with us. But alone or with company we played outside if the weather did not completely forbid, because Father was having his accustomed "Sunday rest."

Arising refreshed from his nap and his reading, he was apt to do a weekly chore which, perhaps because it was pleasant, somehow did not classify as "work" and could therefore be done on Sunday. He would put us children into the spring wagon along with a bag of coarse salt and, after the solid blocks became available, one of them to replace any that might have been used up. In the waning afternoon the horses would amble up the sunflower-lined lane to the second pasture gate. When we were through this makeshift affair composed of three strands of barbed wire attached to two lengths of Osage Orange, our steel-rimmed wheels would bounce over small stones and through the thick meadow grass dotted with clumps of daisies and black-eyed Susans. It was the pasture where the milk cows were domiciled. At last we would come to our destination, the "big pasture," at the other side of the farm.

Then Father would begin laying out the loose salt in a great line, while yodeling: "Co-o-ee, co-o-ee." I doubt if he knew the word "yodel" was in the dictionary, but he well knew how to "call cattle."

At the first note all the proud Black Angus and all the lowly "grade cattle" were on the move. By the time they reached us, they were trotting and bawling eagerly. While they attacked the strung-out salt, Father walked among them, counting and inspecting in the ancient way of animal husbandmen. When he had finished we turned around and drove leisurely back, routing up, perhaps, a pair of cottontails in search of their supper. That was all there was to the trip, but the mood was relaxed and the meadow larks happy-sounding.

There was something about this late Sunday afternoon rite which was deeply satisfying, which seemed to cap off the day properly. It had nothing whatever to do with church, but because Sunday and Church were inseparably linked for us the inspection tour seemed to have a churchly flavor. In good years, that is. In drought years, everything was different, the grass brown by July and the cattle thin. Then Father was silent and there was no frolicking in the spring wagon. Then all I could think was, "Oh God, make it to rain. *Please* make it to rain." Even the meadow larks fell silent.

The old-time Methodist revivals were not of much importance to Belknap life. In order to come into full bloom a revival, whether Methodist or Baptist or store-front, requires a larger community than Belknap. It is doubtful if Billy Sunday himself could have fired up the emotional uprush of a storied revival among us. The neighborhood was too small and remote, and the old-time camp meetings, which would have brought more people into the neighborhood, had been abandoned if they ever existed. And besides, Belknapers were too firmly rooted in their joint sense of propriety for a mass emotion to be easily aroused in them.

Not that the ministers didn't try. Several times, during the years that I can remember, the minister of the time scheduled a week or so of revival meetings. But attendance was poor, limited almost entirely to those who were already of the elect. Usually at some time two or three children nearing puberty would "come forward" and kneel for a time at the altar, while the tiny congregation softly sang, "Just as I am, without one plea," or "God will take care of you."

When I felt that it was my turn to take this step, I took it without any great sense of guilt, certainly no dread of the eternal fires. It simply seemed the right time to take a step which I was expected to take sometime. I was twelve and soon, I had been telling myself in secret, "going to be in my teens." To make the occasion even more right, I had a new dress with tiny red crossbars, which I had managed to persuade Mother to make an inch or two longer in view of my approaching new status. So, "going forward" that night seemed entirely appropriate. I got up from the altar feeling solemn, as children do when they are entering a new stage of life. *"Now I am grown up!"*

But lurking under the solemnity was disappointment.

[103]

Nothing dramatic had happened. I don't know what I had expected, but I did know that Peter Cartwright's converts went bounding around the campground, faces alight and voices shouting, "Hallelujah" and "Praise God." I hadn't the slightest impulse of that sort, not even any of the flooding joy which Grandfather had described so often.

My disappointment led me into some real soul-searching. Was I or wasn't I converted? I questioned myself closely on the point, but nobody else. Either Father or Grandfather could have set me straight in a minute, but I wasn't about to admit that I had maybe been play-acting a bit about the experience to which I had publicly laid claim. Thus the nearest approach to a puberty rite afforded by my family and neighborhood pushed me deeper into secretiveness and separation instead of initiating me into the common experience.

At some time in my childhood whoever happened to be preacher brought in a professional evangelist who had been reduced to small potatoes like Belknap. He let us have it, both barrels and plenty of brimstone. Hildred and I thought his histrionics amusing. Particularly on the night when one of the neighborhood "renters" to whom juvenile snobs felt superior because he had a flock of half-bright children and nothing in his farming operations ever went right, "came under conviction." He was a hulking, gaunt fellow with huge hands and a balding head. His shirt was faded and his work pants frayed at the seams.

The evangelist got him down on his knees and prayed over him passionately. Nothing happened. We sang, "Just as I am, without one plea" over and over, but still nothing happened. The evangelist continued to kneel and exhort, but no light broke. Finally, when closing time was looming, he cried, "Lift up your hands to heaven, Brother, and pray, Brother, *pray!*" Perhaps to his surprise, his struggling sinner did just that. With arms upstretched and head thrown back, he half-sobbed, "Save me, Lord! Oh, save me!"

Knowing that a shared glance might be too much for our facial controls, Hildred and I refrained from looking at each other. But the next day, safely out of paternal earshot, we rehearsed the scene in delight and I made a saucy bet as to how long the conversion would last. After all these years I

[104]

can still see that humble man kneeling at the altar rail, so troubled in his depths that he was willing to transgress his neighbors' sense of the proprieties. It is my impression that they afterwards respected him even less than before. After a while he drifted away to try to make a living from another unproductive farm in another part of the county.

Belknap was not a good field for evangelists. Not only Billy Sunday but Peter Cartwright himself would have had trouble with us. We were a tight little community whose leaders were sober, common-sensical men who believed in working hard, paying their debts, lending a helping hand in a neighbor's hour of need, and bringing up their children to do the same. Outside of Grandfather's dream of sanctification, I doubt if there was even a tinge of mysticism anywhere in the neighborhood.

Even Father, with his compelling conscience and unbending rectitude was a rationalist and undemonstrative in his approach to religion. Making a joyful noise unto the Lord was no element in his religious style. If some one had asked him to put his religious convictions into one sentence, he would undoubtedly have said something about the saving power of belief in Jesus Christ. But he *lived* by Micah's "What doth the Lord require of thee but to do justly, and to love mercy, and to walk humbly with thy God." I never heard him quote Micah. Perhaps he never happened to read the three requirements; certainly it was not a popular text for the preachers of the time. But as he grew older he adopted a formula phrased by a Kansas governor and small-town editor:

"There's so much good in the worst of us,
  And so much bad in the best of us
  That it hardly behooves any of us
  To talk about the rest of us."

It came to guide his own judgments and it made a perfect rebuke to a daughter holding forth on somebody's misdoings — and was undoubtedly good for all our souls. But the spirit behind it and Micah was very far indeed from the rapturous words of David, "Thou makest the outgoings of the morning and the evening to shout for joy," or Isaiah's, "He has done gloriously in all the earth; shout, and sing for joy, O in-

[105]

habitant of Zion"; or Van Dyke's "Joyful, joyful, we adore thee, God of glory, Lord of Love."

It would be many years before I myself could even begin to understand the emotion behind such words and to "translate" them into language acceptable to the science-oriented mood of my century. If anybody in Belknap understand such words, he kept the fact carefully secret.

postscriptum, 1975

As the years slide by, I find myself becoming always more grateful for that small white box of a building and all that it meant in the neighborhood. It gave us not only a sorely needed opportunity for social contact, but the chance to hear the magnificent rhythms of the King James Bible read aloud by another voice than Grandfather's or Father's, and even to stumble through them by our childish selves. I own several of the newer translations and am willing to concede their virtues of accuracy and clarity. But for me the King James, however archaic and inexact, is still the phrasing which comes first to mind.

The unadorned services in that small building helped build in me a sense of the *mystery* of life, and was nourishing to whatever in me was poetic. Such questions as how did the human being get here and was there any purpose in his coming are only partly answered by the sciences.

6

Mamie A. Dungan and daughters Irene, Idylene, Hildred and Avis

More Schools

In time there came a day when I was two months past thirteen and Mother showed me how to pack a trunk. Characteristically, neither she nor Father displayed any pain at the flight of the first fledgling. Long ago they had set their course, and they were not people to flinch when circumstances dictated that the moment had come. Because I was too young to see them as people or to consider that they might be trying to save me distress at parting, their self-control registered on me as indifference. So thinking, I buckled my armor tighter.

More than ten years would pass before I would be permitted to glimpse the toll the departure occasioned. Understanding finally came near the end of one of my annual visits, when Mother said sadly, "Sometimes I wonder if it's a good thing for you to come home. After you're here, I get my life re-organized and the hurting finally stops. Then you're here for a week and I have to do it all over again."

Father and the younger girls drove Mother and me to town to catch the train. How many times I made that trip during the next eight years! Before it there had been the struggle to get my clothes in order, then the packing and the throat-tightening last look-around. Then the long, rather silent trip to town and the wait at the small red station during which my throat tightened still more. Finally, a distant whistle to the east and a black object snaking around the curve in the shining tracks. A conductor bawled "Bo-O-rd" and then there was the instant of desolation. The uncomfortable coach with its pot-bellied stove for winter, its axe for a possible wreck, its limping old "butch" (salesman of candy and magazines) and the spry little conductor, its chugging and soots, its bone-wracking jerks.

Two mortal hours that train took for the fifty mile trip, with stops at five villages, each with its own set of loafers down to see the train come in. Eventually, just as I had resigned myself to spending the rest of my days sealed up in that soul-shriveling tortoise of a train, we would get to Winfield and the young uncle who had come to escort me to my other home.

I do not know exactly why Mother went with me that first time. Perhaps she simply couldn't bear to put me on the train alone. Or perhaps she wanted a hand in buying my new coat and shoes. At any rate she went, and her going greatly cushioned the first leave-taking. I remember her taking me to a shoe store and introducing me to the owner: "This young lady will be in here sometimes. Please try to help her buy wisely." With a delicate accent on "try!"

In some ways the new life was very different. Winfield was a county seat town of around 8,000, large enough to seem like a metropolis after Moline. It had shops on several streets, a sure-enough hospital, even a streetcar line out to the college a mile or so up the Hill. There were no movies in my very first years, but before long Main Street was graced with a small theater. At first it was sans popcorn, but from the start it had a tinny piano and a mixture of the old tunes like

"Take Me Out to the Ball Game" and the incoming ragtime. How wonderful it seemed to see people tripping about in jerky motion through hair curling melodramas.

Dipping into one edge of the town to loop half around the park where Chautauquas and picnics were held in summers was Walnut River, a lazy, high-banked, tree-rimmed little stream whose upper reaches were a favorite rendezvous for hot-dog and marshmallow laden students.

Life itself was different. Marvellous gas lamps and "radiant heaters" with a blue flame flickering over asbestos not only provided more light and steadier heat, but required no disgusting chores like cleaning lamp chimneys or lugging wood and ashes. The house was large, the whole second floor let out to students, three of whom ate at our table and two managed for themselves on gas "hot plates." Their comings and going, plus those of the uncle-student, insured plenty of activity and exposure to the society of young males. To this day I can conjure up, as almost nothing else that happened in those years, the delicious outrage which half-suffocated me when, after one of my early attempts at flirting, the youngest roomer caught me, kissed me hard and then, because I tried to fight him off, spat derisively. Lucky for both of us that Grandmother did not come around the corner just then!

Another change greatly to my liking was what, after the farm, seemed a near-absence of "work." From having been the oldest and therefore invested with a certain existential responsibility, I found myself in a family group where I was the baby — whose commendable deeds were cause for rejoicing and shortcomings ascribed to her youth.

Not much was required of me. I was supposed to run errands, set tables, help with the dishes, and care for my room. The first duty was a delight, the paired chores neither onerous nor rigidly enforced. But on the matter of the room Grandma was adamant. Herself no perfectionist with broom and dustcloth, she proclaimed that I could let that room go until I couldn't walk into it and never a finger would she lift. It never quite came to impassability, but sometimes approached that state before I finally fell to.

My bad housekeeping was proof, if any be required, of the frailty of thirteen-year-old human nature, for this was the first time I had ever had a room of my own and my ego was vastly set up by being able to close a door in the sure knowledge that nobody would open it without asking permission. Not even Grandmother, unless the admonition was especially urgent.

Even though we lived across the street from the campus my chief memory of the early years is of quietness. There was more activity because of more people but not much more noise than on the farm. On warm spring or fall evenings one sat on the front porch and listened to an occasional automobile over on College Avenue and tried to decide if it was a Ford or a Buick; or gave an idle ear to the Glee Club practicing distantly in North Hall or the voices of the returned missionary family across the street or the collegians hurrying up to the YMCA building.

On winter evenings one listened to Grandfather's and Uncle Lish's interminable arguments about predestination and generals until boredom set in. Then one studied or read, with high-buttoned feet stuck out toward the gas heater. It was soon all so usual and so barren of drama that I seemed to myself hopelessly out of things, and therefore compelled to read with desperate greediness in order to discover how things were "out there."

Looking back to those years, I think that for the time and locale the Academy must have been a fairly good preparatory school. Small, to be sure, probably around eighty students altogether. And excessively pious in atmosphere, because most of its students were from "good Methodist homes" which purposed their young to grow up into good Methodists. A few were men already in their twenties and even thirties who had received "a call to preach" and were trying to get ready for college so that they could accept the call. A few came from local families which deemed the atmosphere and quality of education to be sufficiently better than those in the local high school to warrant payment of tuition. Another few came from families which had moved to Winfield with the Academy expressly in mind.

Not long after my graduation the school was quietly snuffed out. Rising standards in Kansas high schools had led to a constantly diminishing enrollment.

The curriculum was fairly classical. In the first year we had ancient and medieval history, English composition and literature, Latin and algebra. The next year we exchanged algebra for plane geometry, ancient for "modern history," and set out to conquer Gaul. No Greek at any time, but enough Latin to let me struggle through the *Aeneid* during my third summer vacation. English, praise be, was with me all four years. The math courses were managed by memorizing formulae and theorems, with the result that I graduated with honors but totally innocent of any math beyond sixth grade, and some of that pretty wobbly. The single science course was physics, offered in the fourth year. Its problems were a curse until I thought to trade them for translations of one of my male classmate's Latin assignments.

Daily attendance at chapel was required of us as well as the collegians, but parts of this hour, such as the "pep talks" before football or basketball games were fun; and some of the "outside speakers" brought us glimpses of life outside Kansas. The numerous religion and Bible study courses were elective, and I did not elect. Sunday School was a place where I could meet girls of my age. Attendance at the annual "protracted meetings" (then "modern" for "revivals") held in the Methodist church just off the campus was not required if I objected that I had studying to do. As a result, the religion-dominated atmosphere was not irksome. I accepted it as I accepted air and water, darkness and light — in the nature of things.

The general piety with which I was surrounded troubled me little. Grandfather still read his daily chapter after breakfast and prayed kneeling beside his chair. But I was used to that and skilled at thinking of something else during any chapter unleavened by narrative. I was also used to being amused by Grandmother's repeated sniffings whenever he got around to one of his favorite chapters, the eleventh of St. Paul's first letter to the Corinthians: "The head of every man is Christ; and the head of the woman is the man . . . For a man indeed ought not to cover his head, for as much as he is the image and glory of God; but the woman is the glory of the man. For the man is not of the woman, but the woman is of the man. Neither was the man created for the woman;

[111]

but the woman for the man." No Woman's Libber could have been more indignant than Cynthia Dungan, born in 1842.

Three of my teachers were really excellent and because the school was so small I had them each year. In all four years I never came upon a time-server. The English teacher, especially, has remained a delightful memory for her perceptiveness, sparkling brown eyes and quick humor. She was a spinster living with and caring for aged parents, but if she ever had moments of feeling "unfulfilled," as her counterparts of today are all supposed to be, her students never glimpsed those moments. As much as any one I ever knew she seemed genuinely to enjoy life. I never listen to the plaints of "deprived" females without thinking of her. Across the years I salute you, Elinor Hayes.

The real joy of those four years was free access to the college library. It probably wasn't much of a library even then and by today's standards would be just nothing, but to me it was riches without shore. When we were reading *Silas Marner* in class, I could take out *Adam Bede* or *Mill on the Floss* and gobble it down almost overnight. Never one to drudge over assignments unduly, I spent most of my evenings with this hit-or-miss, utterly undirected reading. The practice served me well. Because I was always panting to know "how it comes out," I learned to read rapidly. And without that ability and the backlog of indiscriminate reading I could never have survived the English Department of the University of Illinois graduate school.

Another important extra-curricular teacher was Father's sister, Ida, who lived on the edge of town and was in the process of producing red-haired babies and becoming a disciple of Eugene V. Debs. Since she never talked down to me, I acquired some unromanticized sex education to go along with the asterisked silences or pretty notions promulgated in the novels of the day; and since her conversion to Socialism was in contrast to other Dungans, I also learned there is no one true political gospel. Excellent lessons for any adolescent girl to imbibe along with her Latin and algebra.

But the shaping influence in those four years at the Academy was Grandmother, and I know now that the shaping was mostly negative, and that the fault was as much mine as hers.

[112]

When I lived with her earlier, I had rested in her strength and perceived no flaws in her. She had simply been "Granma," refuge in times of family trouble, protector from teasing uncles. But after six years we had both aged. She was now sixty-six and I thirteen, a fact that was in itself a sure recipe for conflict. When we came together again, one of us had fallen out of step with the times and place, and the other was burning to become part of them. Add her refusal to be anything but what she had always been, a country woman made by and for the frontier and my young-snob conviction that anything rural was inferior to everything urban, and the stage was fully set.

By the time she was called upon to endure my adolescence, she had already suffered through seven others, none of which could have been easy. She was also cooking for eight people and caring for a big house at a time of life when most of her contemporaries had settled down to their rheumatism and crochet hooks.

No wonder that by my time she had become a garrulous dispenser of long-spun scoldings which missed being tirades only in their lack of passion or hope of results. "Jawing," her sons called it. When she saw behavior she did not approve, something compelled her to express her disapproval, and when the behavior appeared again the next day, she "jawed" again. When her youngest son was sprouting into manhood, he sometimes threw her into fury on such occasions by stooping to rub coarsening stubble against her face or pulling her down to his knee and trotting her up and down.

I learned to take the wind out of a full sail by acquiescence. "That's right, Grandma . . . Of course not, Grandma . . . I see what you mean Grandma." In one such session she flung out, "Oh, would ye stop agreeing with me, when we both know ye're not going to do a blessed thing ye don't want to."

One of our milder wars was over her conviction that I was old enough to learn to cook. In those days many thirteen-year-olds were about as proficient before the kitchen range as their mothers were. I was not only utterly uninterested in learning to cook but totally unable to deal with "a pinch of this and handful of that" (she never owned either measuring cup or spoons), nor could I put a hand into an oven and judge if it was right for biscuits or cake. Despite all the evidence of her senses, she couldn't accept my disability until one day when I was fifteen she came to the desperate conclusion that it was time I learned to make a pie. At the end of the dreary episode, she capitulated sadly: "Ye're like all the rest of 'em, only book-smart." She was right. Later when I needed to learn and could read printed recipes and use calibrated cup and oven, I made a fair cook. But we went through many a skirmish before she gave up the battle.

I was under Father's instruction, "Get along with her. It won't be easy, but do the best you can." And Mother's, "Be kind to your grandmother. She's always had things so hard." (Never did woman have a more devoted set of daughters-in-law. It was Papa-in-Law they resented.)

So I tried and my methods left a scar. Unfortunately, my ways of "trying" were only an extension of those I had already begun to use at home and in Belknap; avoidance of conflict by putting up a wall around myself and fending off intruders by whatever tactics the circumstance required. Much open conflict was avoided but at the price of forbidding any real practice in learning how to talk things out. At the time I felt that any attempt to communicate real feeling would be futile because she "just wouldn't understand."

At any rate I adopted the tactic of maintaining secrecy about everything that really mattered to me. I had already learned that secrecy's best mask is lively chatter about extraneous matters, particularly if the chatter could be made to strike the funny-bone of intruding elders. At times when secrecy did not wholly succeed in keeping Grandmother out of my sacred precincts, then I evaded or restored to outright deception.

If she was sure the ice on Dutch Creek was too thin, I didn't waste breath in argument but threw my skates out my window and picked them up from outside. When she pressed me to wear long underwear from November to April, I didn't say I just wasn't going to do it. Instead, the first act of my school day during the first year was to go to the "Women's" and fold the offending length of knitted cotton back to above my knees and anchor it there with safety pins until time to go home After the first year Mother yielded to my pleas to leave the longies at home. From then on every time I caught a cold Grandmother was volubly sure that the germs had got in through my practically naked legs and it was a wonder I didn't get pneumonia.

If a class party fell on a blizzardy night, I didn't stay home and I didn't argue. I simply scooted out, planning to take my scolding when I got home. When boys became a consuming interest, I never met head-on her deep conviction that I was much too young to begin "going with the boys." I simply kept them away from her. I didn't want them to meet her anyway or see the inside of her living room. So I met them at the front door, whisked them away quickly and made myself as scarce as I could whenever she tried to talk with me about them.

In all the conflict I had parental backing. "We're on your side," Father would say. "We know she's old fashioned and we trust you to know what is right for you to do. But *try* to get along with her." "And be nice to her," Mother would exhort.

The long scoldings were a bore and a nuisance, but they were the least of my problem. The heart of it was something I never quite faced at the time: I was deeply ashamed of my grandparents. If his *amens* at church embarrassed, her keg-like figure and utter lack of style positively mortified me. In fact, her thick ankles and broad feet came to seem almost indecent. Each year the embarrassment deepened as I came to see my grandparents in sharper perspective.

Like many retired farmers of that era they had brought a team and cow to town with them. Which meant a barn and *smell.* On their vacant lot beside the house, each year they made a good-sized vegetable garden, fertilized with rotted you-know-what. Although a water line ran through the alley, they hadn't bothered to put in running water. A pump brought "cistern water" to the kitchen sink, a windlass drew drinking water from a bored well in the side yard. A pitcher, bowl, and slop jar were part of each bedroom's equipment. In the back yard two little structures set beside the alley line, with stools which set up a steady flush when the lids were lowered. No bathroom, of course.

The interior of the house became progressively more shameful. Each year I suffered more deeply from what Grandmother called "the parlor." Instead of a figured rug set properly on a polished floor, a faded carpet was tacked down. At a time when all Kansas was buying Mission and Golden Oak, the furniture was walnut Victorian, picked up, no doubt, at farm sales and second hand stores. (One of the chairs now occupies an honored spot in my living room!) She even had a "folding bed," a monstrosity which jack-knifed up into something intended to look like a mantel. The extra bed may have been needed in the cramped tenant houses on the farm, but now there was an empty bed in a room just off that "parlor." Why, oh why must she keep on putting herself and Grandfather into that horrible thing, I asked cruel fate. Worse even than its looks was its *position*, beside the window which gave a view and listening post to whatever was proceeding on the front porch. It was, to put the matter gently, a prime stimulus to quick adieux.

In short, the household was hopelessly "country," tarnished me by association, and I felt, most dreadfully handicapped me in my battle for social esteem.

That battle was, of course, no less painful for being mostly in my imagination. I never worried about my clothes. Mother saw to it that my apparel was as good or better than that of most of my friends. But I was considerably younger than my mates. I was also a heady youngster full of bookish ideas which occasionally won me a howl of derision. Above all, I felt in the very core of myself that I was not pretty. Much consultation of the mirror had brought me to the depressing conclusion that my hair was a mousy light brown and my eyes small, gray, and somewhat squinted. Nobody had yet discovered how astigmatic they were. My nose had the Dungan pug. And in spite of all the Cuticura soap and ointment Grandmother urged upon me, my skin was given to pimples and blackheads. Every session before a mirror confirmed my childhood impression that I would never get *anywhere* on my looks.

But as time passed, even while I was lacerating myself over my mistakes and bloopers, I could not help seeing that I was making social progress. By my third year I was on the fringes of what is now known as the "in crowd." By the

[116]

fourth I was definitely in. That was the year when a beau who was later to be a brother-in-law took me out to the countryside on a motorcycle which broke down miles from anywhere. This episode really got me a going-over, for then as now motorcycles were held to be murderous, and then as *not* now the passenger sat in front of the driver, encircled by his arms. To hear Grandmother talk, one would think I was lucky to have escaped both death and pregnancy.

At last, at last I was through with the Academy and into college. What I got out of my freshman year came mostly under two headings: more unrequired reading and the beginning of three friendships which turned out to be lifelong. How different we were from the damsels in Mary McCarthy's "Group" may be gathered from the fact that three of us lived more than fifty years with the men we married and the fourth would have except for her husband's early death.

One was Orra, a wistful green-eyed blonde who read as hungrily as I and felt herself as much an outsider, for she lived at home, her mother having moved from Western Kansas to "put the children in school." Like me, she was handicapped by being neither town nor gown, but unlike me, she was not pert and aggressive in trying to get "in." She was undoubtedly the most reflective of us.

The second was Mabel, who was to be a roommate for two years. In order to come to college she had worked for two years after high school, and to stay in she had to work twenty hours a week in the college offices. She had what seemed an inexhaustible capacity for happiness. Her light-heartedness sometimes helped me to glimpse the absurdity of my quivers and quavers.

The third was Dessie, a handsome raven-haired lass. She never made the honor roll and she never sparkled in conversation. But she carried around enough good sense and practicality to make her an ideal friend for some one not much blessed by either trait. In a way, she was an older Hildred, but her admonitions were more acceptable because they came from someone other than a junior-sibling.

But the reading and the friends were not enough to reconcile me. By the end of my freshman year I was declaring that I simply would not go another year unless I could leave the grandparental home. My ultimatum touched off a family crisis. Knowing that Grandmother would be deeply wounded if I got a room elsewhere in town, my parents offered to send me to the state university. I flatly refused, on the stated grounds that my friends were all in Winfield. I did not elaborate, but my struggle to get "in" had been so hard and my appraisal of my personal attractiveness was so poor that it seemed to me I dared not start over to win myself a place in a new and much larger school. And besides, though a wrecking bar couldn't have pried it out of me, I had some Unfinished Business at Southwestern.

The decision never had to be made. At midsummer my poor time-and-work-battered little Irish grandmother took to her bed and was gone within a week, her body generally worn out, the doctor said. Even then I had the grace to hope that I had not been too great a factor in her weariness. Now I wish that I had not had to wait to have an adolescent granddaughter of my own before understanding how Grandmother must have yearned over me during those years and longed for life to deal kindly with me.

Because I was still with the grandparents, the first year at college was more of the same, even to some of the same teachers. I missed the sharp break which most young people feel on moving from secondary school to college. Because the school was so small, around five hundred students, I already knew all the upper classmen by sight and had even chatted with some who had condescended to note the existence of an "Ac." (As Acs it was never fitting for us to make the first advances.) But I had had eyes to note which girls were popular and what young men counted because of athletic prowess or class office. When one of these spoke or even nodded to me, I was set up for the rest of the day, as indeed any Ac would have been. We had our life; they had theirs. If one of *them* leaned out of the heights, it was only by virtue of his largeness of spirit.

I remember as if it happened yesterday the lightning bolt which went through me one day early in my Fourth Ac year when I came face to face on a stairway with one of the magnanimous ones. He smiled at me, murmured a negligent hello, and went on upstairs. That was all, but Fate had touched down. In my sixteen-year-old sophistication I no longer much believed in love at first sight. But in that instant I *knew* that next year, when I would be a freshman, I would in the current phrase "set my cap" for him — with determination and whatever wiles I should be able to muster. It turned out that he did not get around to notice me until well into my sophomore year. In the meantime campus gossip had him engaged to a statuesque blond whom I detested for being not only in college but, oh much worse, being strikingly handsome.

Moving up to be a freshman raised my status somewhat, but not by much. In those days "'frosh" were kept strictly in their place, which was only a notch or two above that of the Acs. (What balm to first-year ego would have been the phrase "pecking order!" But though most of us were completely familiar with the behavior of barnyard fowl, none of us had ever had eyes to see because no sociologist had yet seen and invented the phrase.)

It never occurred to first year students then to rebel against the collegiate System. We accepted it as the natural order, practically arranged by God Himself. In fact, until my sophomore year, rebellion of any sort was nil on that campus. Things were as they were and as it seemed they always had been and always would be. God was in his heaven, all was right in a world where events flowed into each other without fuss or turmoil, though the Populists had given it a flurry some time back. War, as we read about it in our history books and novels, was an aberration that mankind, or at least the United States, had outgrown. We were freshmen, we would be seniors, and after that teachers or ministers or farmers or housewives or no telling what. In any case, each year we would wax wiser, richer and more important. When our Prexy charged us at least once a week to "look ever onward and upward," we took him seriously, for Progress was inevitable. Whatever changes came to us and our country would be for the better. So we believed, for so did our parents and teachers believe and so did most of the parents and academic mentors of most Amercian collegians in the year 1913.

*   *   *

Meantime, there had been plenty of changes at the farm.

Hildred was in high school. The farming operation had continued to grow. A big square house had been built. Relatives and preachers came and went. Mountains of fruit and vegetables had to be picked and processed. But most important of all, during my third year away, a baby brother had been born and a few days after I left for my freshman year in college, a baby sister appeared. Because of all these events the summers were frantically busy.

By the end of the Academy years I had become the family seamstress — and in those days sewing for a family of four women and two infants could absorb the major part of a summer. Despite Grandmother's intimation that I was hand-stupid, it turned out that I could do respectable buttonholes and blind whipping. So I sewed, just as Hildred cooked, out of inclination. In my case aptitude was wedded to observation: the sewing room was always at least ten degrees cooler than a kitchen where hearty meals had to appear three times a day.

Mother's unexpected pregnancies had touched me in a tender spot. Such occurrences then happened in families with teen-agers oftener than now, but it was still a shock to realize what my parents had been up to. It was a time when it was downright vulgar to indicate awareness of a "delicate condition" and when many women did not "show themselves in public" after the sixth month.

The sight of Mother, the light-footed, walking heavily under her burden was more troubling than the sight of my aunt's similar gait had been because Ida had never moved lightly. Especially in the summer before Marjorie's birth, when I rode regularly in the buggy of a collegian from another neighborhood, I was embarrassed. Mothers of grown-up girls didn't or shouldn't go around having babies. The idea that she could use some comforting words never entered my head and if it had, I wouldn't have known what words to use or how to turn them. As it was, I credited myself with the fact that no word of complaint ever left my mouth. Just as with Grandmother, there was no communication.

The babies themselves soon touched off affectionate interest. And sometimes exasperation, as when the boy-child at age somewhat under two suddenly disappeared from the laundry tub in which he had been cooling himself on the back porch. When his absence was noted, all his sisters set out in search while Mother, too heavy for pursuit, fretted and no doubt prayed. Before long we found his footprints in the dust leading down to the creek. Then we really hurried. So many wheels had been on the road over the bridge that we lost his trail. Two of us ran anxiously up and down the creek, studying the holes carefully, while the third sped up the road. Eventually she met a neighbor in a buggy bearing our naked explorer. The same little guy had a way of tumbling downstairs that summer, his screams at every thump echoed by those of his mother. He also developed a genius for being underfoot when pepper was being transferred from one container to another or boiling jelly poured from pot to glass. When baby sister got to her feet, she too had to be guarded against the more perilous of infantile ambitions. Summers were very busy.

The summer before my sophomore year, when we minded babies on top of all the other work, and I laid down my ultimatum, was dry to the point of severe drouth. While Grandmother died and afterwards, the sky remained its hardest blue, and anxiety moved in upon us.

But the event which was to be really important in the lives of everyone on that farm happened quite unknown to us: an Austrian archduke was assassinated. A few days later in that long, dry summer Father glanced at the front page of his *Topeka Daily Capitol* and commented, "They're at it again," before turning to the market page to see how much the price of his porkers and beeves had dropped in the preceding twenty-four hours, because stockmen were having to flood an already distressed market.

* * *

I came at last to the year of years, when I was a sophomore and every month brought great new experiences, when even I could feel at last I had become part of the life around me.

There were no dormitories on the campus. We housed ourselves as we could, though always with the knowledge that the Dean of Women was keeping an eye on us.

Three freshmen and one sophomore found ourselves renting, each for four dollars a month, two rooms and a bath in the second floor of a house owned by a widow who was helping to put her son through college with the income.

When the four of us came together we were strangers to each other. We were together for only nine months and we never had much contact in later life. But at the time we were unified by our common experience of being really away from home for the first time, free to come and go as we pleased, to be generous and open or closed off to each other.

The phrase "bull session" was still a long way in the future, but we had its 1914 female equivalent. In those days students were not so driven by parents and faculty that the price of such converse was a reason for guilt. For us, the price of late-night chatter was only next-day sleepiness. It was no price at all in view of the fact that three of the four of us that year began to date our future husbands. Nobody was there to make us go to bed, and whenever did collegians keep decent hours if not compelled to?

So we talked and talked from our nice-girl, romantic selves' limitations. Any freshman of today would be awed at our naiveté. When we got onto the pros and cons of "spooning" we were all of the opinion that a little hand-holding was all right, but *kissing* should wait for engagement. We had been advised that fellows passed along to each other the names of girls who kissed easily and gave them a reputation for being "fast" — a fate from which all of us shuddered away.

But even in the late night when confidences and speculations were easy there were some which I did not share. The statuesque blonde was out of school that year, but the earlier campus gossip made me wary.

For me the real events of the year happened outside the small, placid circle in which I lived. The friendships that counted for the long haul were not with my roommates. But the fact that each evening I came back to these guileless young women who accepted me as they thought I was and expected me to do my share of room-cleaning and no more than my share of bathroom occupancy, formed a kind of cushion for me. In a sense, they were my family.

The story of the year must be considered against the backdrop of that particular campus in the school year during

[122]

1914-15. Much of it, therefore, now seems unreal, even to me.

First of all, it was a very small school. By November everybody would know everybody else and nothing, literally nothing, could happen without becoming instant common knowledge.

Second, it was a school in Kansas, a state which would keep its prohibition law on the books for another thirty-five years and which in 1914 was completely Victorian in its posture on manners and morals. Finally, it was a Methodist school. Its Board of Trustees was composed of prominent Methodist ministers and a sprinkling of well-to-do farmers and businessmen. At least three-fourths of the students were from Methodist homes.

There was no drinking, no dancing, no late-night card games, and no cars to spirit students away from campus restrictions. If there was any obscenity I never heard it. (However, among all of today's outpouring of four-letter words I would then have known the meaning of only two — so some may have gone over my head.) Even smoking was furtive and never by females. It was a school which had always been run on the lines laid down in the Puritan ethic and the Methodist Discipline.

In only one department had a crack appeared in the solid facade of nineteenth century Methodism. Fifty-five years after the publication of *The Origin of the Species* a slender young biology teacher had begun, very gently and cautiously, to introduce the idea that maybe creation was a much longer process and otherwise quite different from the one described in the first chapter of Genesis. He had drawn around him a group of students who after some initial sparring had accepted Darwin's theory, thereby entitling them to consider themselves enlightened, modern thinkers. The situation made the Board of Trustees uneasy. They were rumored to have spies in the biology classes and may actually have had them, for several fledgling preachers were reputed to be taking the courses as a test of their faith.

Sex was, of course, not considered a fit subject for study. The only courses in which it was openly discussed were biology and botany, and then having to do with humans only by implication. The English Department used expurgated texts

[123]

of Shakespeare, and practically all the assigned novelists were Victorian, equipped with asterisks as needed. Not for us were Balzac or Oscar Wilde. Advanced German classes introduced us to the plays of Hauptmann and Schiller, but the juicy portions were never discussed or even translated in class. Naturally, Faust did not come our way.

Although most of Freud's basic work was already done, our psychology teachers stuck to Thorndike and James. I took every psych course available and in my senior year was an assistant to one of the two teachers, but I was out of college before I met up with Freud and his immediate disciples. Nor had Einstein, that other foundation-shaker of the early twentieth century, appeared on the campus. Physics classes were grounded on the tidy universe of Newton and Faraday.

The college was just what our eloquent Prexy often declaimed it to be: "A place for Christian education, a place where high character is formed, where men become strong and women remain pure." Toward the end of the year some of the more unregenerate of our little group derived an absurd amount of pleasure from hearing my Knight of the Stairway mimic the presidential rhetoric, even to the peculiar way the last word came out "pew-ore," with rising inflection.

Besides the formidable list of no-no's, there were by today's standards some sad deprivations. We had brought with us to the campus no cars, no guitars, stereos, radios, or tape recorders. We had for our edification no radical speakers or writers — probably not more than a dozen of us had ever even heard of the day's No. 1 radical, Eugene Debs, or read a line by Upton Sinclair or the muckraking journalists led by Lincoln Steffens. So we hadn't the excitements of despising the System and organizing demonstrations against it.

As for drugs, there weren't any, not even alcohol. Some of the "wilder" males may have occasionally got hold of some beer, but most of us hadn't even tasted it and would have spat it out in distaste if it had touched our tongues. Hard liquor was never around. Perhaps two or three of the more literate of us had come across the word "hashish" in our reading, but that was the closest any of us came to the hallucinatory drugs.

Any student of today, confronted with that list of prohibitions and deprivations would wonder what on earth we did for entertainment. We went downtown for an occasional movie. And, like all young people, we flirted and we fell in love, both prime sources of entertainment. (In those days rare was the person who graduated without being committed.)

We also talked in long, groping sessions whose basic articles of faith were very far indeed from those of the world we would have to inhabit. We went in groups or couples to Dutch Creek for wiener roasts. We went to intercollegiate athletic contests, after whipping ourselves into a frenzy of "college spirit" so that the emotional release of the hoped-for triumph would be maximum. We joined such organizations as the Y's and various Glee clubs and a Drama Club which put on occasional programs. One play was considered daring because at the end of the last act the hero actually kissed the heroine!

Fraternities and sororities were forbidden but we had our version of them, two "societies" for men and two for women. Males were either Athenians or Delphians, females either Belle Lettres or Sigma Pi Phi's. Athenians and Belles were linked in social bond, Delphians and Sigmas. Each pair had a meeting room set aside for it in the College and there one evening each week, each society repaired to have a business meeting and put on a program of music, "readings" (usually very dramatic and accompanied by well-rehearsed gestures) parliamentary drill, or whatever the program committee had arranged.

In the fall as freshmen were registering, leaders of the societies carefully looked them over. A little later came a furious rush season, when a young man with athletic ability, good singing voice or some other obvious social asset was besieged. Parties and picnics were then the order of the day. Also, carefully planned foursomes, in which the rushee's blind date was the most ravishing Belle or Sigma available. Until the rush season was over, life was hectic. Once a student made his choice he was of course immediately dropped by the other side.

He was also expected to live by his choice. If it was Athenian, the chances were that he would confine his attention to Belles instead of wandering off after the fleshpots of Sigma Pi Phi. Between the two paired groupings there wasn't much

[125]

fraternizing, except in athletics, which bound everybody together against the common enemy. I wouldn't say that the line was drawn as sharply as that between the Capulets and Montagus, but it was a line. In our more honest moments we knew that we were being silly, but most of the time we were disdainful of the other side and at its every transgression asked ourselves loftily what could we expect anyway.

For what reason I cannot remember, I chose the Sigmas. Maybe the Belles had better fish to go after that year. Or maybe I chose because my uncles had been Delphians — or even because I knew that He of the Stairway was a Delphian. Dessie and Mabel were Sigmas. Of the three of us, only Mabel had anything to do romantically with an Athenian — a proportion of miscegenation about typical of the entire school, I imagine.

* * *

My freshman English teacher had been an alumnus of the school who had gone elsewhere to take a Master's degree and was now back making a little money before going on to Harvard for his doctorate. He was a crisp, no-nonsense type who was death on spelling and grammar errors and great on the advantages of outlining one's ideas before starting to produce the weekly "theme." The readings assigned were mostly to illustrate expository, narrative or argumentive writing. (Yes, Virginia, that was the way the textbook described its organization.) Nobody got excited about that course, although I liked it because I liked to write, even when protesting loudly against having to do it. And how was the teacher to know that I muddled my piece around to the point of satisfaction or despair and *then* made the outline which must accompany it?

The first English class in the sophomore year was, therefore, a shock. The new man was Emery Neff, who was later to make a name for himself at Columbia University. When we met him he was a slight youngster of around twenty-three, whose sandy hair and fresh complexion made him appear even younger. He, like his predecessor, had a Master's and was taking time off from graduate studies to garner some experience and money. As it turned out, he got plenty of experience and not much money.

[126]

He was very young, this Master from Columbia, very Eastern and not very cool in his approach to anything. Though he was too urbane ever to have confessed that he wanted the experience of living for a time in the cultural outback, something of that motivation must have brought him to us, for a budding academician of his promise could have found a dozen better-paying jobs in the East.

In those days the sophomore English class was a "survey course," where students were led in quick dips through the principal English writers, beginning with Beowulf and ending with Matthew Arnold. Naturally this meant that we read many snippets of poetry. For the first time I was in contact with some one who loved it passionately and could read it well. That fall I was tinder for any flame, and the experience went deep.

Beowulf was no torch, because the effort of translation was too much. But Chaucer got to me. I was hooked from the minute I heard Neff read the opening lines:

> *Whan that Aprill with his shoures soote*
> *The droghte of March hath perced to the roote,*
> *And bathed every veyne in swich licour,*
> *Of which vertu engendred is the flour;*
> *Whan Zephirus eek with his sweete breeth*
> *Inspired hath in every holt and heeth*
> *The tendre croppes, and the yonge sonne*
> *Hath in the Ram his halfve course yronne,*
> *And smale fowles maken melodye,*
> *That slepen al the night with open ye,*
> *(So priketh hem nature in hir corages):*
> *Then longen folk to goon on pilgrimages.*

It seemed to me I had never heard such musical expression or such true feeling for the very essence of Spring. Because the anthology we used had been put together so discreetly, even the Miller and the Wife of Bath were reasonably decorous. But I had brought with me from the Academy the habit of reading around such assignments. As a library assistant that fall I was being taught the rudiments of cataloging, but the stack copy of the complete *Tales* interested me so much that I pored over them until I could read the archaic language in quick guilty gulps while at work, then take them home at night.

Such response from a student always nets him special attention. Before long the ardent young teacher had appointed himself my reading guide and was inspiring me to try my own hand at verse-making. He may well have been amazed that such as we could be found in what must have seemed to him a cultural desert. The excitement of the discovery, his zeal as a new teacher and his youth all inspired him to the fatal mistake of asking some of us if we would like to form an English Club, in which we would read and discuss some of the *recent* literature not included in the regular course but still, he thought, "important for college students of today to be familiar with." Not many would be invited, he enticed, only a select few who were really interested.

Of course the idea caught on. By November we were meeting regularly.

Meantime, He of the Stairway, who had the unromantic name of Harry, was among those who also responded to the new teacher. Along with his athletic skills he was genuinely attracted by intellectual achievement. He and the brilliant, lonely young Easterner were about the same age and they became friends. And as even intellectual young men do, they gossiped about girls. What more natural than the teacher should recommend one of his sophomores as an interesting possibility for acquaintance?

Two years after the discharge of electricity on the stairway, I had my *chance*. But, I also already had a date for the suggested evening. After a week or so came second chance. Once again I had promised to go elsewhere and was too bound by the campus code to break my promise. I was sure that he would never try again. Who of the football elite would risk a third rejection? In the bull session that night I beat my breast and vowed to turn down all invitations for the next month.

After a spell of anxious waiting, I was finally called again — and this time, oh heavenly joy, I was free. It happened that we shared the English Club adventure.

Another couple involved in it was Dessie and her young man, Howard White, later to be a political scientist of some renown. Orra, too, was a member. In all, around a dozen of us began to meet and discuss samples of "modern" literature chosen for us by Neff. When it fell to my lot to review

[128]

The Doll's House in one of the first evenings, the slammed door set up a great commotion in my eighteen-year-old heart. Never would any man make a doll of me! Though why I thought any would try, I cannot now imagine. The two generations of pioneer Kansans back of most of my male acquaintances had never been able to afford the luxury of doll-wives. Their women had to *work!*

Also early on the agenda was *Man and Superman,* which seemed to us simply crackling with revolutionary ideas. *The Importance of Being Earnest* was another of the early blockbusters. As can be imagined, for a group like us to read and "discuss in mixed company" such plays was a very heady experience. How *avante garde* we felt!

Meantime the new teacher had been so indiscreet as to use a regular instead of a bowdlerized text in his Shakespeare course. Unluckily for him, a member of the class was a girl whose minister-father was a Trustee. Campus gossip, based on fact or not, had it that when she failed one of her first tests, she was moved to show the text to her father. Naturally he was horrified. And naturally, knowing his duty, he straightway carried to the president the foul stuff Daughter was being forced to read.

About the same time gossip about the newly formed English Club began to seep into Prexy's office. Then what tumult! Almost every member of the group was called in to be quizzed about its activities. Somewhere Prexy got a copy of *Man and Superman* and read it with the hair stirring on his scalp. It has been one of my husband's lifetime delights to recount that *he* was asked to explain how a young man from a home such as his could possibly have brought himself to review in mixed company "a play which makes a lecher out of me and every other married man."

The reply was also a source of endless delight. "Jesus said, 'As a man thinketh in his heart, so is he,'" explained the dissenter, 1914 style.

From there, he always later claimed, the interview proceeded to some length, neither party condescending to raise his voice or budge from his morally superior, Biblically-fortified position.

But the crown of the remembered delights has been the

report brought back from a later faculty meeting by our sympathetic professor of German. There, tattled "Heine," Prexy announced that Carlson was thinking beyond his undergraduate status. Meaning: "Carlson is too big for his britches and so will bear watching." And so he was. That spring he and a few other unregenerates formed the PPP Club (Pitch, Pinochle, and Poker) which met a few times to play penny-ante in an unfurnished room under the very chapel itself.

Next, word got around that Neff had taught his student-friend to smoke. The president of the campus Y.W. marched in to tell Prexy that she knew for a fact that the young man in question had smoked long before he ever saw Neff. (She did, indeed, for she was engaged to his older brother.)

Dessie and Howard were summoned for separate interrogations. Orra was not called in, but in spite of her timidity asked for an interview so that she might defend herself and her friends. After all these years I still occasionally wonder why I alone was never on the carpet. Nobody sent for me, and characteristically, I lay low. Aunt Ida, however, took it upon herself to go under a full head of steam, demanding to know if I was thought to have been guilty of any indiscretion. She was assured that there was no smallest blemish upon my fair name.

Throughout the whole comic episode no personal opprobrium fell on any of us. The Administration held to the lofty position that it was merely seeking to protect us from a corrupting influence. After all, the entire lot of us were from homes which expected the college to keep us in sound condition.

For two weeks or so the campus buzzed and nobody talked about anything else. Not even a winning basketball team could take the spotlight off us. Before long the Trustees met and our teacher was out of a job.

An innocuous spinster was hired to fill out the term. Neither she nor we did anything to make the other's life fruitful during the four months she was with us.

But Neff had done his work. Not one of us ever settled down again to an exclusive reading diet of the old fare. While we were prohibited from meeting on an organized basis, what one of us discovered was passed on to the others, so that *Leaves of Grass* (what a shocker that was!) *Hedda Gabler,* more Shaw, some H. G. Wells and much else circulated among us. Neff had taught us to read the book review sections in the library magazines, and the good old Everyman edition made many books available to us at prices we could afford. One could make a strong case for the argument that the best thing the Administration ever did for us educationally was to remove Neff and force us to explore on our own.

Looking back at the episode from today's perspective, I think the really remarkable thing about it is that not even among ourselves did we raise the cry of "academic freedom." In fact, I don't know that any of us had ever heard the term. Certainly it never occurred to anyone to paint a sign or organize a protest or even get up a petition. We simply swallowed our outrage as best we could. But never thereafter were any of us much impressed by the then current view that wisdom and authority are synonymous. And because the whole operation had been carried out under cloak of a religion-based concern for our morals, almost every one in the group began to examine the religious views by which authority claimed legitimacy. It was an enormously maturing experience for all of us.

*　　*　　*

In each of my four years it was my good luck to have a quite different living experience, so that in each of them I had to make a different kind of adjustment. The shift from living with the grandparents had been radical. In some ways the junior year shift was even greater.

Five of us — Dessie, Mabel, a pair of sisters named Hamilton, and I — rented what amounted to a furnished house for the year. It is still a matter of some wonderment to me that a school so carefully watchful of student behavior should have allowed us to set up such a menage. Three of us began the year engaged, the older Hamilton girl speedily became so, and the younger was the most popular girl in the freshman class, a real little charmer. If anybody — Dean of Women, Dean of Men, or Prexy himself — ever cast a suspicious eye upon the arrangement, we never knew it.

So there we were, maintaining a home for ourselves, feeding our beaux on many occasions, entertaining them whenever they showed up (which was often) until whatever hour they departed, trying to keep up our grades, running ourselves ragged with campus activities, all without benefit of *any* chaperone. If that is hard to believe, consider that the rent for a place with kitchen, dining-room and living room, bath, and two large bedrooms was fifteen dollars a month, three dollars for each tenant. I know, because I recently came upon a batch of cancelled checks among some of my father's papers.

Another remarkable feature of our situation was how little friction it engendered. We got through the year with almost none, partly because I, the only fractious one of the lot, kept a tight rein on myself, but mostly because the group elders, Mabel and Dessie, set us down the first day to make a house-keeping schedule. The kitchen assignments, I well remember, decreed that we cook in pairs, each pair to make its own menus, do its own shopping and clean up after itself. I was Dessie's partner. Because she could cook and I was handy about setting tables and scrubbing potatoes, we got along equably. On Saturday morning we all hopped to and before noon had done our laundry and cleaned the house — and in the process extracted a now unbelievable amount of solid fun from our chores.

The only source of even light frost among us was money. Every Monday morning we each put a dollar and a half in the food kitty. The sum was supposed to cover the week! The trouble, when there was trouble, was that the first-of-the-week cook teams tended to overspend, so that the end-of-the-week teams sometimes had to fall back upon beans and cornbread, which naturally constituted grievance. Cooking in those days, even on our sketchy basis, was very different from a time of instant potatoes and canned or frozen everything.

An old snap-shot of us, recently blown up for the amuse-ment of children and grandchildren, shows us dressed up in our Sunday-best. Our high shoes, floppy big hats, ankle-length suits, and wide white collars are guaranteed to con-vulse, but the really funny feature of that old picture is the expression on our faces. All of us are smiling, with a mixture of coyness and smugness, at a world which that year seemed all strawberries and cream. The German U-boats were prowl-

[132]

ing and Woodrow Wilson was squaring off to get himself re-elected because he had kept the country out of war. But the faces of the innocents posing in Lord's Day finery announce their confidence that the skies would smile on them forever. No wonder children and grandchildren look at us in awed laughter. The only picture which could be funnier would be of us in gym or basketball uniform of middy blouse and full black bloomers — the latter ever so daring because when we were running, they showed our knees.

With so much dating going on, the question of who had the living room on what nights might have become acute, but we managed that also without friction by setting up a rotating schedule. On any given night couple Number One had the living room; Number Two the dining room; Number Three the kitchen; Four the porch swing, weather permitting. Weather not permitting, Four went with Number Five to a movie, provided the gentlemen had six-bits for admission and street car fare. If not, they went for walks or to the library for study.

Early in the year Dessie and I realized that if we doubledated and did our spooning together we could each have the living-room twice as often. In fact, we had the best of the whole arrangement, because we were never reduced to walking. Howard had a horse and buggy that he used for transportation from his home at the edge of town to the college. That year he was editor of the school newspaper and I was assistant editor. On the night when we were scheduled for the porch swing or a walk three of us would ride in the buggy down to the newspaper office to read proof and set up heads and later be joined by a fourth for a dish of ice cream. (Cokes were unknown then.)

Other blissful hours were spent canoeing by twos or fours on the Walnut River, Harry having come into ownership of a canoe. Surely no hours can be more idyllic than those spent by lovers drifting between the high banks of a small stream. Or *safer* — canoes were not made for carnal transactions.

Academically, it was a good year. I became interested in psychology and continued to read German classics under the direction of a really good teacher who had grown up in a German-American home. Our "Heinie" would soon be out

[133]

of the teaching profession because German would be dropped from curricula everywhere during the rage of hate for all things "kraut." But that year, when I needed him, he was there.

The new English teacher was a middle-aged woman, a true-believing Methodist and very conservative in her literary tastes. She won our grudging respect, however, because of her genuine concern for our development and her own real response to the portions of English literature deemed to be proper materials.

But the best academic gift of that year was a course in the history of Western thought, taught by a man who in spite of a handicapping stammer, could make Plato and Locke relevant to 1915-16. My guy was also in the class and usually we studied together. The great trio, Truth, Beauty, and Goodness, burst upon us at the same time. Because we had heard about Goodness all our lives, though mostly in terms of do's and don'ts, it did not flame for us like the other two. How seriously we pondered Keats' words about truth being beauty and beauty truth! What did they mean? Were they to be taken literally?

Both of us had grown up in households where truth was not only much talked-about but equated with veracity. ("Tell me the truth. I'll stand for anything but lying.") Now as we read and talked, the word broke free from such confines. We had learned the year before that custom and conventional morality sometimes obscure it. Now it became a far-beaming light toward which man can move, but which he can never hope to reach once and for all. Partly because of those meandering, kiss-sprinkled conversations as we tried to puzzle out the meaning of the philosophic writings selected for us, the concept of Truth always thereafter had a very special meaning for us.

Beauty was even harder for us deal with, because the philosophers hooked it to "the aesthetic experience," a phrase neither of us had heard — although I, at least, had had vicarious contact with it in the joy Mother took in a brilliant sunset or the first flowering cherry tree in the spring. Neither our homes nor our college had afforded us any training whatever in the graphic or the dance arts and not much in music.

Neither of us had ever set foot in an art museum or heard a symphony orchestra or seen a dance troupe. Only in the "great" English plays and poems had we felt something of what we supposed the aesthetic experience must be. I, at least, tried vaguely to make the Kansas prairie and woods surrounding Walnut River supply what I supposed the philosophers to be talking about.

We began to examine, as much as we could, reproductions of paintings our books discussed. In those days the art of color reproduction was unborn, but we could get something from sepia prints when we studied them for the qualities which were said to make the originals great. The books which came our way never got around to mention Gauguin, Van Gogh, Cezanne or any other of the great painters of the late nineteenth century whose best work was already two or three decades old. Even so, we learned something. Though we didn't know it at the time, we were laying the foundation for a joint life-time which would be spent in trying to get ourselves an education.

Emotionally, of course, it was a tremendous year. Much more than in the previous year I felt myself one with my house-mates. My teachers fed my ego with special attention, and my peers, while wise enough never to entrust an office to me, selected me for work on the school paper and year-book, and seemed to enjoy the stories or jingles the program committee prodded me into concocting for the amusement of sister Sigmas.

And beyond all else, I was IN LOVE. True, I still knew next to nothing about loving. But I was up to my ears "in love" — dizzy with it, doubly giddy with the knowledge that my feeling was reciprocated. No wonder I soared up the Hill on the wings of morning and floated back down in ecstatic weariness.

The first adult love affair is a great means of growth. I was only nineteen, but I recognized this as adult love, partly because of what it was doing to me. A Herman Hagedorn poem I read that autumn helped me to understand and has stayed with me through the years:

> *I wandered down the dusty street;*
> *Men jostled there and wept and swore,*

But in the throbbing and the beat,
The Babel of the feverish street
Was something that was not before.
Deep into each pale, passing face
I gazed in wonder. What strange gleam
Had in this gray and sordid place
Clothed as with glory each pale face
And lit dim eyes with dream?
Like an explorer, midst those eyes
By unimagined deeps I trod:
And lo! where yesterday were lies
And lusts in those world-hardened eyes,
I saw the stars of God.

Not much as poetry, but at the time a great shedder of light.

Up to that year I had said saucily that I liked persons, not people. Because my young man liked people also, the tight bands about me began to loosen slightly and some of my careful defenses to soften. The change was nothing like complete, but it was a beginning.

There were only two flaws in that year of 1915-16.

One was that under the press of my other activities I was scamping all class assignments but those in poetry and philosophy. For the first time I was hitting the high spots and having to cram intensely at exam time. I knew I was doing it and kept nagging myself to do more studying, but there weren't enough hours in the days and evenings. The result (perhaps!) was that for years after graduation I often had a nightmare in which I was going to a "final" for which I was unprepared. "This time they're going to catch me," I would agonize all the way to the ordeal. And sure enough, when the questions were spread, not one of them could I decently answer. Waking would be bliss.

The other flaw was dread of the coming separation. The year skimmed by, bringing us relentlessly to its end. Always before I had wished time away, so that I might begin to "really live." Now I clutched at it and tried to hold it as one holds savor, by concentrating on its quality. But the more I tried to hold it, the faster it seemed to go, and the less endurable the prospect of separation seemed. As preparations for the graduation exercises for the class of '16 came on, I watched in dread. Three months it would be, at a minimum. More likely four and a half, because he had contracted to teach next fall in his home town while helping to put out the winter wheat on his family's Western Kansas holdings. No weekends were likely until at least mid-October.

The days dwindled, then the hours, and soon he was putting me on my clacking little train. Four months were a third of a year. Practically forever. Our homes were only about two hundred and fifty-five miles apart, but in those days the trip had to be by train and would require twenty-four hours or more each way — a block of time which no wheat grower could afford in the frantic summer months. I did not kid myself. It would be at least four and a half months. There were no tears, but my throat tightened into pain and choked me into silence.

Since I remember little about that summer, it was no doubt like all the others, hot and work-filled. I recall it as a time when I fought a losing battle to keep fourteen-year-old Idylene from reading the letters which arrived two or three times a week, no matter how furious the pace of wheat harvest. Hildred was wiser. She recognized the battle as foredoomed and simply turned her letters over to our romance-sniffer. Only lately did I discover that the pest also sneaked such modern gems as *Madame Bovary* from the bottom of my trunk and carried them up a ladder to the attic for undisturbed perusal.

When September came again, it ushered in another very different kind of living, though in the same house as the year before. Dessie was out for a year. Of the previous year's five only Mabel and I remained. The three new girls were strangers and not engaged or even dating — "old-maidy," Mabel and I labelled them in the privacy of our room. Very few young men ever visited. Mabel was a good cook and, naturally enough, I was her helper. Once again I learned nothing about the art, insuring that I would marry without it.

It wasn't much of a year academically either, for I was finishing out the thirty hours of education courses required for a certificate to teach in Kansas. Dull stuff, all of it. And worse, what any student would now damn as "irrelevant." I didn't use the word, but despised the courses. However, they were a requirement for teaching, and my parents thought I should have a certificate in case I ever wanted or needed to teach. So I took them dutifully and maybe learned something in them.

Old English was required for my major. Also dull, of course. I already had twice enough German to satisfy the language requirement, but I had somehow acquired the notion that knowledge of French was an important item in the educated person's equipment and I aimed to be educated! Alas, half the class were freshmen athletes working off *their* language requirement in French because of a campus myth that it was easier than German. (No Spanish was offered, though we were almost on the outer-reaches of the Southwest where Spanish was even then a second language.) With no interest whatever in the course, no language "sense" or even a decent base of English grammar, the freshmen pulled the class down to the level of sluggish drill. How bored we seniors were, sitting there listening to the mumbling and stumbling from the back rows!

I remember two things about that year with some degree of sharpness. One, of course, was the weekends when Harry was in town after being on a train all of Friday night. Another encounter with Time. First, counting off the droning weeks, then the days, and finally the hours. At last he was getting off his train and I could be fully alive again for thirty-six hours, in which I was again trying to tether down Time. He came, I think, three times during the winter, though perhaps only twice, and then again for my graduation.

The other sharp memory is of the day in April when Chapel was given over to the Declaration of War that was in the headlines that morning. Like most students of that or any other day, we had been reading only headlines — and not even those with any regularity. For us, Europe was a backward and bloody continent which periodically, so our history books told us, churned itself up to a war. Up to now the current sample of this deplorable European habit had seemed unreal, of no concern to us. But that April day when Prexy read a chapter, prayed, and talked to us solemnly about the great change which had come, each of us began in his own way to take in the fact that our own, our most personal lives were to be taken over. Because it would take a while for the Army to get organized, Prexy told us, he strongly advised young men, especially seniors, to finish out the college year instead of rushing out to enlist.

While he was talking, I looked at my male classmates sitting about me. Could they really be going out to shoot other young men? And some of them be shot themselves? My friends. And my Beloved. The habit formed in childhood took over: *Oh God, protect him, and Howard for Dessie and Merb for Mabel. And all these about me.*

When Prexy had finished we shuffled out of the room silently. For none of us would life ever be the same again.

postscripta, 1975

> Every time I read of a new book burning in West Virginia or some other where, I am reminded that at least we of the English Club had our episode sixty years ago. It couldn't, I think, happen in any Kansas school now.
>
> I have never felt cheated by the small, religion-dominated

college into which I gravitated. If, knowing all that I now know about coming events, I had it to do over, would I accept my parents' offer of the state university? Probably not. I brought out of Southwestern several lifelong friendships and a husband who turned out to be one of the world's best. Plus a desire to *know* that has forced me to prowl the libraries of several cities.

Moreover, almost all our teachers were good human beings who took an interest in their students and extended themselves to sharpen our desire to know. In that time and place a college professor's concern with his students was undiluted by the edict, "publish or perish." Intellectually, the English Club episode was probably the best thing that happened to us in our whole four years. And because it couldn't have happened at Kansas University, I'm inclined to think that, even had I been clairvoyant, I would still make the same choice that I did at age eighteen.

*　*　*　*

A few days ago I was scandalized to note in the St. Louis Post-Dispatch that golden oak folding beds (of, no doubt, the very vintage I detested so heartily) are now bringing up to $300 at antique sales! I had already observed that cast iron tea kettles, such as the one I fussed at Grandmother for keeping when she might have a near-weightless, brightly colored *new* enamelled kettle, have moved right into the living room's fireplace ensemble. And cream cans — those loathsome objects which had to be thoroughly scalded out on the hottest of days — are prized collectors' items. For all such I have no nostalgia whatever!

*Harry G. Carlson
in photo
taken June 1916*

7

The Wedding

Weddings are usually a time of confusion, but few achieve the wild muddlement of mine. Because it has become something of a legend among younger generations in two families, it should be described with whatever accuracy can now be summoned after all the tellings and re-tellings.

To begin, it was the occasion for no great joy in either family. The Carlson parents had barely met me, but were well aware that I was neither sturdy of body nor sedate of spirit, clearly a somewhat risky choice for their Scandinavian son. My parents approved of my young man but utterly lacked enthusiasm for my marrying *any one* before the ink had dried on my diploma. They had sacrificed to give me my "chance," and experience had instilled in them the conviction that a female college graduate can find better scope for her energies than marriage -- a state, which in their experience

[141]

meant, both soon *and* late, babies. Besides they argued truthfully, I was very young. A year or two of teaching would season me, indeed would earn me a right to marry. They themselves had waited years for the right time.

These were reasonable views. But I was crazy in love, I had already been separated from my love for a year, and there was a War on. Whenever did parents win in that situation? By the time of my graduation, it was conceded in the family that there would be a summer wedding. After all these years I applaud them: once they had yielded to my determination, they did their best to put aside their disappointment and not to spoil my last summer at home. But I knew, how well I knew, they wished I had been willing to wait at least a year. From the knowledge came a sense of guilt and, from that, tension. If either they or I could have attempted communication, the gap might have been bridged. But none of us knew the right words or found the right moment. The two months between commencement and wedding were probably the loneliest two months I would ever know.

By the first of June, graduation time, plans began to shape. By then we knew that Harry was not going to be drafted. In spite of his four years on a college football team, a never-repaired hernia classified him 4-F. But his younger brother, who had already assumed management of the farms, got by the Army doctors with flying colors. Some one would have to take over the wheat acreage which Woodrow Wilson was already beginning to say would be an important factor in Victory.

Later in the month more lines had appeared in the emerging picture. Howard would go into OTC as soon as he had collected his Master's degree at Kansas University. He and Dessie would be married whenever they could fit it into his training program. Mabel was to be married when Merb finished OTC.

After all our double dating, it naturally seemed to Dessie and me that we couldn't possibly be married without each other's presence. But how was that to be possible when both grooms would be so up-to-their-ears in their patriotic duties that they might not be able to get off for even one wedding?

[142]

And how could Mabel and all our other friends living near or in Winfield be on hand? These were very solemn questions.

Dessie and Harry came to see me graduate. After much discussion we hit on the idea of a double wedding. It would be in Winfield, and of all places in the Sigma-Delphian meeting room, which with extra chairs would accommodate nearly a hundred people. We would transport our families to Winfield for the big day. Lesser decisions followed rapidly. I would wear my graduation dress and Dessie would have a duplicate made. We lined up the wedding party, engaged the hall, decided to have two ministers, and asked Cleo Hamilton to play the wedding march and her fiance to sing — if, of course, he could get away from camp. Everything but the date was easily arranged.

The three of us studied a calendar. June was out — both bride-grooms were unavailable. July would be difficult because of wheat harvest and the uncertainty of a three-day pass at that stage of OTC, not to mention the fact that the brides' fathers would be furiously trying to get their corn "laid by." So it would have to be August. On account of the pass, it must be on a week-end. So we put a pencil down on the first Sunday in August, that year the Fifth.

It was of course, a hare-brained plan. Why both of the brides' mothers failed to put their feet down I cannot imagine, except that a new War addles lots of brains, not all of which are young.

But even as we studied the calendar a totally unplanned clock was ticking. Mother had come on for the graduation and was annoyed by a nasty little hack she had developed. It wasn't much, but it was persistent and it seemed to get more importunate with each passing day. By the time we had been home a week it was steady enough to confirm her worst suspicion. Small Brother had joined her in a busy warm-up for whooping cough. Another week and Hildred had entered the chorus; later, Idylene and, finally, Baby Sister.

I had never had it.

In those days pertussis serum wasn't even a gleam in a researcher's eye. One got the disease and one wore it out or died in the process. The incubation period might take ten days; what our trusty old "doctor book" called the "catarrhal

[143]

stage" lasted a week or more; the middle stage lasted a month to six weeks. Lying in bed those hot June and July nights in Southern Kansas, I used to listen to a solo, or chorus, and shudder. How fearfully I checked off the incubation periods! But just as I would get safely through one, another victim would begin to grow noisy and red-eyed. Even arithmetic as frail as mine could predict that the wedding ceremony might be rudely interrupted.

Add to all this apprehensiveness a more than usual share of the usual farm-woman summer work because three of the four of us were ailing; then add in the struggle to get together some kind of trousseau in a time when slips, petticoats, dresses, even panties were mostly made at home — and one gets a picture of my June and July. It is understandable that I did little worrying over a war in which the youth of Europe was being slaughtered and into which my classmates and friends were being propelled. There is a limit to what one person can worry about.

When, finally, at the end of July the last of the infectious periods were over, another peril menaced. I fell into what Grandmother D always indelicately called "the trots" — which everybody knows to be a very unhinging malady. Nowadays, probably my trouble would be labelled an allergy, perhaps to peaches, of which there was always a God's plenty on that farm in the last days of July. By whatever name, it was nothing new for me. Every midsummer I had to deal with it for a while.

But this was no usual time. Mother, bless her, recognized the gravity of my plight and had Hildred crank up the old Model T and take us to consult the doctor. He promptly ordered up a big round of castor oil. For the first time in my life I took the nasty stuff willingly, and swallowed it back down until at last my outraged stomach accepted it.

By Wednesday evening, August first, I was able to begin upon Mother's standard first-meal-after-washout: dry toast and potato water. Naturally, I was weak, but at such a time, if ever, spirit can dominate body.

The family was to drive to Winfield on Saturday. I had duties there that day. So on Friday afternoon I took the train to meet Dessie and help my aunt get ready a wedding breakfast for Carlsons and Dungans. I thought that everything that *could* happen had happened.

Saturday morning dawned hot and clear. By ten o'clock a strong Kansas wind was searing a countryside that hadn't felt rain in a month. Later, I knew in retrospect that the day was more than hot and windy. It was what Father called a "weather-breeder."

At the time I was in no condition to notice weather. My aunt's household was frantic that Saturday morning. Hildred, who was famed in the family for angel food cakes, was to bring three of them for the breakfast. But a lot of other things were supposed to come before cake, in quantity to feed twenty-five people. The helpfulness of three children, aged nine, seven, and three can derail an ordinary social event. These kids had a WEDDING in their midst, and were naturally under every foot and ruffling every hair. Somebody, perhaps the bride herself, washed out her white silk hose and hung them out to dry. When they were brought in, the lady of the house stood in the middle of her kitchen and with her black eyes snapping besought heaven just to please let her know *who* could possibly be so ignorant as not to know that wet white silk turns yellow in the sun. Socialist or not, she could still get her Irish up.

It was quite a morning. I even managed to scorch the sheer white organdy in my dress, although luckily under an arm, so that if I remembered to keep my hand down, it wouldn't show.

But the first real temblor of the day did not come until about noon when a boy on a bicycle delivered a telegram.

The groom had been spending the summer on a wheat-and-cattle farm which he and a partner were buying from Carlson *fader*. They jointly owned a two-passenger Model T, but in those days nobody put much confidence in Stuttering Liz as a mode of long-distance travel on roads which might be blanketed in six inches of dust or slashed with six inch ruts or, in case of rain, just plain impassable. So my groom had driven eleven miles into a little Western county-seat town south of Dodge City and caught the train which once each day huffed and jerked eastward, picking up passengers and cream cans and stopping at every crossroad blessed with a

[145]

grain elevator. Twelve hours later and 170 miles away, after a "layover" in one of the villages, the train would arrive in Winfield. At some time during the long, jolting morning, it had dawned on my beloved that he would get into Winfield after the court house had closed. In 1917 such requisites as pre-marital blood tests and three-day waits were unheard of, but *no license, no wedding.* So at one of the villages he got off the train and wired me to get a license.

I was furious, to the point of good old Dungan-type explosion. Whoever heard of a bride getting the license? The county clerk would think I was having to drag the guy to the altar or maybe even that this was a new version of a shotgun wedding. In the whole two years of our relationship I had never been really angry with him. Now on the day before I was to marry him, I simply boiled. Why hadn't he bought that license, I raged. He must have driven past the courthouse every time he had been in town all summer. Was he ashamed to have his neighbors know what was afoot?

Eventually my aunt and uncle got me calmed down enough to perceive that I was only wasting energy — if I wanted to be married, I must go purchase the license. The uncle took me downtown, and his presence helped to make the transaction seem less indecently female.

All went well until the clerk asked me what the G in my Darling's name stood for. I said I thought it was "Gustavus." The official explained paternally that a marriage license is a legal document and it had to be right. Now it had happened that every time I had asked said darling about that G, he had smirked and claimed that his name was Harry Gustavus Adolphus Carlson. So I really didn't know for sure. The upshot was that the amused official offered to keep the courthouse open until after the train was in.

At six Uncle met the train and conveyed the groom to the courthouse. It was lucky for me that I had cooled off considerably. Very lucky, indeed, for when it was the groom's turn to be asked what *my* middle initial stood for, he had to say that he didn't know. The understandably irritated official, who had waited late as a favor, suggested testily that somebody really should introduce these two young people! A telephone call brought the information that there wasn't

[146]

any middle name — I had simply an initial because everyone else seemed to have one and I wasn't going to be shorted. With sure fore-knowledge that I would be twitted all the rest of my life, I eased out the last of my wrath and helped to get a big family-reunion meal ready for the table.

By this time we were expecting families to appear at any minute. My family had planned to start at mid-morning. Even with time out for a picnic lunch along the way they should have covered the fifty miles by mid-afternoon. The Carlsons were leaving in early morning and should, we calculated, have done their 200 miles by six o'clock.

Because fear of road accidents had not yet become imbedded in the human nervous system, I cannot remember worrying about the delay except in terms of the rehearsal Dessie and I had planned for the evening. Being very modern young women we were not to have ourselves "given away," but we did plan that a brother of each groom and a sister of each bride would be in the ceremony. One of the ministers had warned us that it would be well to have a small rehearsal Saturday evening. Therefore, it was important that the families get into town in time for bridesmaid and best man to remove dust and perspiration, eat and get to the rehearsal. At some time in the evening Hildred would also need time to ice her cakes and press the lovely soft-green dress she would wear on the morrow.

About seven the bridal pair went down to Orra's home, leaving directions that when Hildred and Frank appeared they were to follow. Dessie and Howard were already there. Amid many giggles and a few fairly serious thoughts as to what the words in the back of the hymnal meant, we went over the responses together. When the missing attendants still had not appeared, we all went out to the back yard for tennis. But because it was an August evening in Kansas and we were more excited than we really knew, tennis could not last long.

About the time we were back in the living room, my father appeared at the front door, something obviously very wrong. His movements were stiff and his voice unnatural. There had been an accident, he got out. Ten miles out of Winfield. The young children and the wedding guest were unhurt at

[147]

my aunt's home. The rest of the family were in St. Mary's Hospital.

On the way to the hospital we learned, little by little, what had happened. The roadmakers of that time had a fad of grading the dirt roads up to a sharp peak in the middle, so as to get better drainage. Because a stiff south wind had blown all the dust over onto the west-bound side of the road and because no oncoming traffic was in sight, Hildred had pulled over into the dustless lane. At a sudden, imperious honk behind her she had swung the wheel too fast and too far. The car had rolled over, then half over again and landed upside down in the ditch. A crowd of local people and passersby soon gathered. Hildred was screaming wildly, Idylene completely out. (Later Mother told me that Father himself had been so dazed that he simply went off and sat down, leaving her to cope.)

When the men had turned the car back over, they found its engine still running. Somebody had driven it with the unhurt passengers to my aunt's home. The only vehicle in the vicinity that could transport an unconscious girl and her mother to a hospital was a *hearse!*

When we got to the hospital we found Hildred sitting up in bed still hysterically trying to control the car and wailing that she had killed one sister and spoiled the other's wedding. Idylene was unconscious with what the staff doctors said was a serious concussion. Characteristically, Mother had held up until they were all in the hospital with nurses and doctors in charge. Now she too was out. Both she and Father had cracked ribs, and numerous contusions were beginning to show on all four of the injured.

It was quite a stroll the bridal pair had down that hospital corridor.

*　　*　　*

About ten the resident said that Idylene was showing signs of improvement and Aunt Ida, ever ready to take charge, told me to go to her home and get some sleep — she and Harry would stay in the hospital. The decision turned out to be about the worst which could have been made, for she would have been infinitely better able than I to cope with what happened the rest of the night.

Shortly after I got to the house, Grandfather managed to get the curtains in his room on fire. Still the incessant reader, he had been sitting as usual at his desk with the gas lamp nearby. In order not to miss any stray breeze in the hot sticky night, he had picked up the window curtains and draped them over the lamp arm. He had done this scores of times. It never happened before and it never happened afterwards, but that night it did. When Uncle and I heard his agonized shout we ran in and helped put out the flames, but not before they had consumed the papers on the desk and a good part of the skin on Grandfather's hand.

Hardly had that emergency passed than the neighbor-guest who had been unhurt and apparently calm, went into delayed hysteria over her near-disaster. All the rest of that long night she wept over it, agonizing over her selfishness in leaving husband and child forlorn while she set off to have a good time, wailing over the thought that she might never get back to them, moaning that the car was going over, OVER.

It was my first experience with pure hysteria and I hadn't the foggiest notion of what to do. I tried comforting. I tried cajoling. I even tried to exert some authority. But she continued to carry on, *all night!*

And just to add a final touch to the doings of that desperate night, when some impulse sent me into the room where Small Sister was sleeping, I found her lying in an open second story window whose screen latch was loose. One good childish flop and she would have crashed to the concrete walk beside the house.

About five o'clock, just as daylight began seeping in, the hospital watchers came home with word that Idylene was definitely better and that my parents said they would be able to come to the ceremony if we decided to go ahead.

But before any decisions, I pleaded that something had to be done for our guest. Aunt Ida put her head into the door for an instant before making for the telephone. Feeling very green and foolish, I presently watched a doctor take out a needle and give the poor woman peace.

By this time it was beginning to rain, a light, gentle rain that grew slowly more purposeful — the kind of rain that Kansans ordinarily welcome as a gift straight from the hands of God. Now it only added further difficulty to an occasion already gone hopelessly awry.

In the end we decided to proceed. We really hadn't a great deal of choice. There was no way to notify all the numerous people who would soon be dressing for the wedding. Howard and Dessie would be married, with or without us, in order to make their mid-morning train. And besides, after all this calamity, who would ever have the nerve to plan another wedding?

By the time the guest was asleep and the decision made, the *day* was upon us. A cousin was drafted to take Hildred's place, even to wearing the green dress and hat. My uncle went to the hospital to get my parents. Aunt Ida sailed full steam into the sadly delayed preparations for a wedding breakfast. The red-headed children were anywhere and everywhere, always at the most inopportune moment.

After a time Father and Mother arrived, walking very stiffly and still somewhat groggy from their sedatives, and because of the cracked ribs unable to get hand to head. Who helped them dress? The bride. Who scrubbed and decked-forth small brother and sister? The bride.

Meantime, though he didn't tell me about it until later, the groom had entered a hell of his own. He was not by nature a worrisome person but he hadn't been asleep all night, and bridegrooms are notoriously given to agitation. Perhaps the rain was also a factor. At any rate by this time the devastating thought had occurred to him that lightning does occasionally strike twice. *What if the missing Carlson family were also in some hospital!* He was already in a first class stew when he opened the box in which his suit had come from the cleaners. (He had decided not to buy a new suit but simply to have his good blue cleaned.) As he lifted out the contents he lost all remnants of his Scandinavian cool. The trousers were not his and they not only didn't match the coat, they were a good three sizes too big. It was Sunday, no shops were open. And the fatal hour was closing in on him. Frantic telephone calls located a pair that might do — navy blues belonging to the teen-aged son of the minister who was to marry us. There was a run through the rain to get them. The trousers turned out to be practically as tight as the skin God had bestowed, but the groom couldn't be choosy. So he had to go through the ceremony in mortal terror of splitting out his borrowed raiment.

Meantime, I had finished dressing my parents and the children, and time was closing in on me too. As I gathered up my trousseau underwear and yellowed silk stockings, a vast wave of self-pity hit me. A girl's wedding day was supposed to be the biggest, the happiest day of her life, wasn't it? Sitting on the edge of the bathtub, I felt my throat tighten and my stomach convulse. In another instant, experience warned, the flood would loosen. Luckily, my vanity overcame my self-pity. All that had happened was bad enough — was I going to add to it by getting my eyes swollen and my nose blocked? For the first time in my life, and almost the last time, I drew a cold bath and went into it with a fortifying gasp.

The Carlsons still had not arrived. In his panic over their absence, the groom added to his woes by forgetting the license and ring and had to go pelting back through the rain after them.

At last we all were in the hall, only twenty minutes late. Father and Mother were seated rigidly in the front row with the two youngsters. The White-Pope contingent were on the other side of the aisle — not a single fluster had marred *their* wedding preparations. Did they live so much better than we, I wondered dismally.

Upwards of a hundred people settled themselves and the musicians went to their work. Then, just as a tenor voice began what was then a newish song, "I Love You Truly," and Harry was considering what friend he could nab at the very last moment to serve as best man, the Carlsons came puffing up the long series of steps that led to the main college building. After the ceremony we would learn that the rain had begun in Western Kansas just as they were leaving home and had moved along with them at just about a Model T pace.

In 1917 there were not more than a few miles of paving or even gravel on that whole two hundred miles. Afraid to stop for fear they'd mire down, they had slippped and sloshed, slogged and lurched through a tormenting day and night. No one in that family had slept either! (The brunt of the

[151]

ordeal was borne by a brother's wife who was six weeks pregnant and had to spend a week in the hospital after she returned home.)

Frank was shoved into line and handed the ring and with only a word of whispered directions from the ministers, we were ready. Somebody signalled the pianist to begin the *Lohengrin* and the procession began to move.

At that instant a curious thing happened to me. A blessed calm descended. All the mishaps and all the apprehensions faded, leaving only the nearest to quiet joy I have ever experienced. For me, it was a beautiful wedding. For the groom, however, the relief of his family's arrival still left his painfully tight pants as a subject for worry.

But even for me the moment of joy was fleeting. Ahead of us lay a trip to the hospital, where Idylene tried and failed to recognize us, and we tried and probably failed to convince Hildred that she had not spoiled the wedding.

Then followed the breakfast. There was little joy in *it*. The place being Kansas and all participants Methodist, there was, of course, no champagne. But nothing that comes from a bottle could have livened up that group of half-dead people. The food, to quote my aunt, had had to be "slapped together" and the table "set any old way." (The cakes never got iced.) Two of the important members of the party were absent and one of those present was so nauseous from her prolonged car trip that she could barely look at the food. The sedated guest dragged herself numbly to the table. Dungans and Carlsons in their fatigue struggled to make a good impression on each other. If ever there was a wedding that was not *celebrated* ours was it.

Any soothsayer, knowing all the events preceding the wedding and beholding the two families' first introduction to each other, would have pronounced the marriage to be ill-omened, if not positively doomed.

In fact, however, it turned out to have great survival value. I still had to learn how to think "we" — first in terms of two persons, then of a family, then two small cities, then three large cities, and finally the human species. My father would die in a few months. The War and wheat-culture would engulf us, then the Depression, then another War,

and still more Wars, and change so vast and all encompass-
ing that *nobody* could even imagine it. But under all the
hammerings of life we would both continue to live — and grow.

Having come of age on the tranquil side of 1917, we
would deal somehow with the turbulent side of that water-
shed year.

postscriptum, 1975

A marriage beginning in such confusion and near tragedy
could not really be expected to promise much in the way of
solid durability. This one, however, lasted until the groom's
death almost fifty-three years later, and was the richest relationship either of us ever experienced. In the beginning there
were tensions, of course. But the relationship cushioned all
difficulties (even the Depression) and sweetened all triumphs.
Whether we were in Urbana, Wichita, Washington, Phila-
delphia, St. Louis, or on a loved white Gulf beach in Florida,
the relationship was the warp upon which all our weaving
went forward.

In recent years, when the hand dealt me is so nearly
played out and the feminist ferment is abroad in the land, I
have often wondered if I would have been happier had I con-
centrated on a career instead of insisting on having a family
and being involved in civic affairs. The answer I always come
to is, "'Probably not." Unlike so many of my contemporaries,
I do not feel estranged from the life around me. I may not
approve of all that goes on in it, but I am in and of it —
and I love both many of the actors and the show itself.

INDEX

ABOUT THIS BOOK . . .

Various sizes of Baskerville Roman and Italic types have been used throughout the book. The paper is ivory Carnival offset, 70-lb. The printing was by off-set lithography. Binding was done by the Zonne Book Bindery of Chicago.

In the world of books, unusual incident occurs more frequently than in the world of commerce generally. Fine book manufacture demands personal and careful intercourse between all the principals who combine their talents in the making of a book. In choosing the illustrator, Ward Schori of Schori Press was familiar with Herschel C. Logan's work in woodcuts. Mr. Logan's Kansas scenes have won wide attention, and awards, for their authentic and distinctive handling. Mr. Schori commissioned Mr. Logan to do the art for SMALL WORLD, LONG GONE and sent the artist a set of galley proofs.

In reading the galleys, Mr. Logan relived his own Kansas boyhood of more than half a century ago as he read the author's chapters: *The Child; The Family; The Farm; The School; The Church.* When he got to the chapter, *More Schools,* he was amazed to discover that Avis Dungan had attended Southwestern Academy and College, in his home town of Winfield, at the same time he was a high school student there. The SMALL WORLD, LONG GONE, suddenly was as fresh as today. Half a century later he discovered they were townsmen in their youth, neither knowing the other existed until this book was published, yet sharing many family contacts during that earlier day.

For the most part, the photographs remain untouched, indicating the limitations of the period and the fond handling they have received since.

Richardson Hall, Southwestern College, Winfield, Kansas